Lent by Heart

How to Memorize the Gospel Stories of the Passion and Death

Learn One Verse a Day
For the Season of Lent

Books by Heart™

Bill Powell

BLUE VINE

First edition 2013.
Printed in the United States of America.

Lent by Heart, version 1.1.

Published by Blue Vine Books.

To order this and other **Books by Heart**™ directly from the publishers, please visit: BlueVineBooks.com

Cover design and typesetting by Wineskin Media: WineskinMedia.com

ISBN-13: 978-0615823867
ISBN-10: 0615823866

The cover of this book was laid out using *GIMP*.

The text was composed in *markdown*, edited with the text editor *emacs*, and converted to various formats with *pandoc* and *calibre*.

The text of this book was set in Lato and Palatino, using the LATEX macros and LATEX packages, especially *memoir*, with the TEX typesetting engine. The output PDFs were previewed with the PDF reader *evince*.

These programs are professional, open source, and free.

Cover artwork includes elements courtesy of:

lostandtaken.com
spiritsighs-stock.deviantart.com

The ornaments throughout the book are in the public domain, provided courtesy of: openclipart.org.

This book includes the **Books by Heart**™ lessons, version 1.2. These lessons have been adapted for this text, to help you memorize the Passion.

For Sharon and David

*And they gave him to drink
wine mingled with myrrh.
But he took it not.*

Mk 15:23

In this book,
    you will learn
the Passion and Death of Christ,
    from the Gospel of Mark,
        by heart.
You will hear and feel the rhythms,
    imagine the scenes,
        and renew your memories.
By the end of Lent,
        you'll know these words by heart.
But your memories of the Passion
    will have only begun.

Contents

Learn the Passion During Lent

"What are you doing for Lent?"

I've dreaded this question since childhood. At this time of year, with Christmas long gone, you'd think that finishing up winter would be bad enough. But no, we have to go and pick some grueling sacrifice. For six and a half weeks. Right at the slushiest, grayest, grimmest part of the year.

Even more difficult than choosing a sacrifice can be figuring out why, exactly, we're doing this. Over the years, I've collected various explanations for this ancient custom of self-infliction.

Some sermons delve into the mystery of redemptive suffering. Others run the opposite direction, exhorting me to do something positive for a change.

Then there's the "resource management" approach. No TV means an extra hour (or more) for prayer. No morning doughnut means extra money in the poor box. These economical arguments can't be the whole story, but they do tug deeply at my dutifully hyper-developed sense of efficiency.

And what about the historical angle? Not too long ago, early spring was simply the hungriest time of the year. This was a question of weather, not theology, and was just as true for the Iroquois as for the Italians. In a stroke of liturgical genius, the Church turned this obligatory fast into a meaningful ritual.

(Although it's also true that the weather in the hungrier parts of the modern world doesn't quite sync with this European seasonal rhythm.)

The Two Goals of a Lenten Sacrifice

I don't claim to understand the full meaning of the Lenten sacrifice. But I do think this season has *at least* these two simple goals:

- We want to make an *effort*. We want to do something new, that we don't usually do.

- We want to make this effort so that we can get closer to Christ.

To meet these goals, I believe I've found the perfect sacrifice. **Every day during Lent, you learn a Bible verse by heart**. But not just any Bible verse. The story of the Passion. For instance, the Gospel of Mark, chapter 15.

During Lent, you can learn one verse each day from the fifteenth chapter of the Gospel of Mark. By Easter, you'll know the entire Crucifixion and Death of Our Lord by heart.

(If you prefer to learn the stories of the Passion from another Gospel, I've included those verses as well.)

Why is learning Scripture by heart a perfect match for Lent? Two reasons.

You're Ready to Make the Effort

First, the effort. Memorizing takes effort. Period.

But don't let that discourage you. This book shows you how to *minimize* this effort. If you've tried to memorize before, try to forget that pain, especially if you had to do tons of repetitions, or imagine lots of bizarre mental pictures as "mnemonics".

In this book, you'll learn natural methods like finding the **rhythm** in the verses, and strengthening your **imagination** of what's actually happening in the scene. Learning by heart can (and should!) be pleasant.

But even at its best, learning takes effort. It takes time. You're training a new skill, and that means forming a new habit.

What better time to train than Lent? We're already geared up for precisely this kind of project. Hopefully the effort is mostly a pleasure, but if it gets a bit difficult, well, it *is* Lent.

Built-in Daily Time With Christ

There's a second reason to learn the fifteenth chapter of Mark during Lent. Unlike ditching chocolate or even adding a daily rosary, learning these verses automatically helps you think about Christ.

Yes, self-denial and prayers have major spiritual value. But it's one thing to try to imagine Christ while you repeat Our Fathers. It's quite a different experience to *say the words* of the Bible, to tell those stories. It's easier to think about what you're saying, because you're always saying something new.

Also, for a time, you'll say these words every day. Now, don't panic! Telling the verses doesn't take long, and you won't have to do it every day forever. In fact, these daily recitations become built-in daily meditation time.

You don't have to choose a Lenten sacrifice, and then *also* figure out some way to "enter more deeply into the season". When you learn the Passion by heart, you think about Christ every single day.

How This Book Will Help You Learn the Passion This Lent

This book includes two major aids to learning the Passion this Lent, plus a **bonus feature**.

First, you get the **verses of Mark 15**, typeset as **rhythmic stories**. Although you could learn the verses from any Bible, this book uses a **visually memorable** layout. Instead of blocks of prose, you see these words with rhythms that move like poetry.

This gives each verse a more unique look, and also helps you **speak** and **hear** the verses with rhythm. They become much easier to remember.

Second, you get the **Books by Heart™ lessons**. These lessons will show you, step-by-step, how to remember a long text like Mark 15. These lessons form the core of this book. They've also appeared in other books in the series, such as *Christmas by Heart* and *Easter by Heart*.

The bulk of these lessons are the same in every book in this series, because all these books focus on memorizing the same kinds of texts. But in each book, I adapt certain examples and discussions for the particular text we're learning. In this book, we'll focus on Mark 15 and the Passion.

You can read the whole book at once, but the lessons are also designed so that you can read one lesson a day. You start learning one new verse a day right away, and the lessons gradually tell you what you need to know as the days pass.

As a bonus feature, I've also included **rhythmic verses** for the **Passion stories from the other Gospels**.

If you'd rather learn a different Passion narrative this Lent, you can make that choice.

Or, for future Lents in the years to come, you can **use this book again** to learn other Passion narratives. You'll find these stories at the back of the book.

I use the Douay-Rheims Challoner version for the all the Scripture in this book. This old translation will probably remind you of the famous King James version. Although the DRC presents some challenges, it also has features that make it a great choice for memorizing. I explain these features in a later chapter.

Let's begin with a slow, thoughtful reading of Mark 15.

The Stories of the Passion from Mark

Here are the forty-seven verses you'll learn this Lent. They tell the story of Christ's Passion and Death, from the fifteenth chapter of the Gospel of Mark.

You'll be coming back here every day, so while you're here, **bookmark this page.** Keep one bookmark here, at the beginning, and move another bookmark forward each day to your new verse.

For now, as you read these stories for the first time, **don't think about memorizing**. Just read. Many words and phrases will be familiar, but expect to be surprised.

Mark 15: Good Friday
Condemned by Pilate

Mark 15:1

Pilate questions Jesus

And straightway in the morning,
    the chief priests holding a consultation
with the ancients and the scribes
    and the whole council,
binding Jesus,
    led him away
        and delivered him to Pilate.

And Pilate asked him:
    Art thou the king of the Jews?
But he answering,
    saith to him:
        Thou sayest it.

And the chief priests accused him
    in many things.

And Pilate again asked him,
        saying:
        Answerest thou nothing?
Behold in how many things
    they accuse thee.

But Jesus still answered nothing:
    so that Pilate wondered.

Pilate's festival custom

Now on the festival day
 he was wont to release unto them
one of the prisoners,
 whomsoever they demanded.

And there was one called Barabbas,
 who was put in prison
  with some seditious men,
who in the sedition
 had committed murder.

And when the multitude was come up,
 they began to desire
that he would do
 as he had ever done unto them.

Pilate offers to release Jesus

And Pilate answered them
 and said:
Will you that I release to you
 the king of the Jews?

For he knew that the chief priests
 had delivered him up out of envy.

But the chief priests moved the people,
 that he should rather release
  Barabbas to them.

And Pilate again answering,
 saith to them:

What will you then that I do
    to the king of the Jews?

But they again cried out:
    Crucify him.

And Pilate saith to them:
    Why, what evil hath he done?
But they cried out the more:
    Crucify him.

And so Pilate being willing
    to satisfy the people,
        released to them Barabbas:
and delivered up Jesus,
    when he had scourged him,
        to be crucified.

Crucifixion

Mark 15:16

Jesus is tortured

And the soldiers led him away
    into the court of the palace:
and they called together
    the whole band.

And they clothed him with purple:
    and, platting a crown of thorns,
        they put it upon him.

And they began to salute him:
    Hail, king of the Jews.

And they struck his head with a reed:
    and they did spit on him.
And bowing their knees,
    they adored him.

And after they had mocked him,
    they took off the purple from him
        and put his own garments on him:
and they led him out
    to crucify him.

Jesus is crucified

And they forced one Simon
    a Cyrenian,
who passed by
    coming out of the country,
the father of Alexander
    and of Rufus,
        to take up his cross.

And they bring him into the place
    called Golgotha,
which being interpreted is,
    The place of Calvary.

And they gave him to drink
    wine mingled with myrrh.
        But he took it not.

And crucifying him,
    they divided his garments,
casting lots upon them,
    what every man should take.

And it was the third hour:
    and they crucified him.

And the inscription of his cause
    was written over:
        THE KING OF THE JEWS.

And with him they crucify two thieves:
    the one on his right hand,
        and the other on his left.

And the scripture was fulfilled,
    which saith:
        And with the wicked he was reputed.

Jesus is reviled

And they that passed by blasphemed him,
    wagging their heads and saying:
Vah, thou that destroyest
    the temple of God
and in three days
    buildest it up again:

Save thyself,
    coming down from the cross.

In like manner also
    the chief priests,

    mocking,
said with the scribes
    one to another:
He saved others;
    himself he cannot save.

Let Christ the king of Israel
    come down now from the cross,
        that we may see and believe.
And they that were crucified with him,
    reviled him.

Jesus dies

And when the sixth hour was come,
    there was darkness over the whole earth
        until the ninth hour.

And at the ninth hour,
    Jesus cried out with a loud voice,
saying:
    Eloi, Eloi,
        lamma sabacthani?
Which is, being interpreted:
    My God, My God,
        Why hast thou forsaken me?

And some of the standers by
    hearing, said:
Behold
    he calleth Elias.

And one running
    and filling a sponge with vinegar

and putting it upon a reed,
    gave him to drink, saying:
Stay, let us see if Elias come
    to take him down.

And Jesus, having cried out
    with a loud voice,
        gave up the ghost.

And the veil of the temple was rent in two,
    from the top to the bottom.

And the centurion
    who stood over against him,
seeing that crying out
    in this manner
        he had given up the ghost,
said:
    Indeed this man
        was the son of God.

Women who looked on

And there were also women
    looking on afar off:
among whom was Mary Magdalen
    and Mary the mother
        of James the Less and of Joseph
            and Salome,

Who also when he was in Galilee
    followed him
        and ministered to him,
and many other women
    that came up with him
        to Jerusalem.

Burial

Mark 15:42

Joseph of Arimathea

And when evening
    was now come
(because it was the Parasceve,
    that is,
        the day before the sabbath),

Joseph of Arimathea,
    a noble counsellor,
who was also himself looking
    for the kingdom of God,
came and went in boldly to Pilate
    and begged the body of Jesus.

But Pilate wondered
    that he should be already dead.
And sending for the centurion,
    he asked him
        if he were already dead.

And when he had understood it
    by the centurion,
he gave the body
    to Joseph.

Jesus is buried

And Joseph, buying fine linen
    and taking him down,

wrapped him up in the fine linen
   and laid him in a sepulchre
      which was hewed out of a rock.
And he rolled a stone
   to the door of the sepulchre.

And Mary Magdalen
   and Mary the mother of Joseph,
      beheld where he was laid.

You're going to learn all that by heart. Let's get started!

Books by Heart: Passion and Death

Now we begin the Books by Heart™ lessons, which will show you an easy method for learning these verses by heart.

You may have already read a similar version of these lessons in another book in this series, such as *Christmas by Heart* and *Easter by Heart*. But in this book, I've adapted certain examples and discussions for Mark 15.

You don't have to read this whole book on Ash Wednesday! Instead, you can do **one lesson per day**. Read the first lesson, say the first verse, and then it's up to you how quickly you read the other lessons.

Speaking Out the Verses

Every time you say a verse, you want to:

- **Speak out**: Speak **loudly** and **slowly**, with **rhythm** and **expression**.

- **Take it in**: As you speak, **see** the words as they are written, **hear** the words you say, and **feel** the **rhythms** and the **shapes** of the words on your tongue.

- **Experience**: Let the words lead you to **imagine the scene** in this **story**.

Seem like a lot to remember? Don't worry, we'll be going over all this in detail. You'll always see critical points more than once.

In this first lesson, you'll learn how to **speak out** the Gospel. Speaking out is the crucial first step. You have to speak a verse before you can **take it in** and **experience** it.

Speak Out

You're used to reading silently. But in ancient times, they were used to reading out loud. Words were *spoken*. And the first step to learning these stories by heart is to **read the verses out loud**.

Read the verses out loud:

- **loudly** and **slowly**

- with **rhythm** and **expression**

Loudly

How loud? **Loud enough to hear yourself.**

Don't mumble. When you mumble, the words only happen inside your head.

You need to be loud enough to *hear* your own words, as if someone else were talking to you. Hearing the words will activate additional mental processes, and lead to stronger memories.

You always want to **activate as many different kinds of learning as possible**. Each kind of learning has its own set of **mental connections**. The more connections you make, the stronger your memories.

Slowly

Don't rush! When you're first learning new verses, speak slowly. Not *painfully* slow, but a little slower than you usually talk.

In normal speech, we slur past common words. Here, you want to **pronounce every sound in every word**.

Rhythm

The Bible has rhythm! Unlocking these rhythms makes the verses both come alive and stay in your mind.

As I mentioned earlier, I've typeset these verses like a **poem**, instead of the usual prose paragraphs. Here's the first verse:

And straightway in the morning,
    the chief priests holding a consultation
with the ancients and the scribes
    and the whole council,
binding Jesus,
    led him away
        and delivered him to Pilate.

You're looking at one of the best-kept secrets about the Bible. **The Bible has rhythm.**

Oral Culture

The Bible was written in an **oral culture**, a culture that largely depended on the spoken word. Human speech has a natural, loose rhythm. In an oral culture, speakers make these rhythms even stronger.

They organize their thoughts into words and phrases that play off each other, back and forth, rising and falling. Their audiences *expect* these rhythms, listen for them, and remember them.

In our culture, we associate rhythm with *entertainment*: nursery rhymes, popular music, rap. Advertising jingles.

Our serious work *avoids* rhythms. Doctors don't want to sound like Dr. Seuss.

But oral cultures *depend* on spoken rhythm for serious work. Jesus preached in rhythm. The Gospel writers composed with rhythm.

Free the "Verses" Back Into a "Poem"

You want to **speak** these verses with **rhythm**.

Almost every Bible translation imprisons these verses into long, solid columns of compressed text. But why do we call them **verses**? Don't verses mean a **poem**?

Poems never translate well. Most rhythm, like rhyme, is lost in translation. But if we listen to our Bible translations, especially an older translation, we can still find the **back-and-forth rhythm** of the phrases.

The first modern scholar I know of to unlock these Bible rhythms was Marcel Jousse, a French priest in the early twentieth century. In 1925, his book *The Oral Style* revealed that beneath the prose of the Gospels, even in translation, the phrases rise and fall with strong rhythms.

Back and Forth Rhythms

Let's look again at our first verse, Mark 15:1. Normally, that verse would look like this:

And straightway in the morning, the chief priests holding a consultation with the ancients and the scribes and the whole council, binding Jesus, led him away and delivered him to Pilate.

But I've freed these words into a more natural, back-and-forth rhythm:

And straightway in the morning,
    the chief priests holding a consultation
with the ancients and the scribes
    and the whole council,
binding Jesus,
    led him away
        and delivered him to Pilate.

Do you hear how the phrases interlock? One phrase rises, creating tension. The next phrase falls, resolving the tension.

And straightway in the morning ... the chief priests holding a consultation

What happened straightway in the morning? The chief priests held a consultation.

This rise and fall, question and answer, is much stronger in some places than others. But even the more prosaic sentences can be broken into short phrases and spoken with rhythm.

Speak With Rhythm

Every verse in this book has been set with rhythm. As you read, use the layout to help you see and speak these rhythms. You'll usually see **couplets** and **triplets**.

The first line of this **couplet** rises, creating tension,
    The second line falls and resolves the tension.

The first line of this **triplet** rises, creating tension,
    The middle line begins to fall,
        But only the last line resolves the tension.

Sometimes, you'll see a set of four lines. I'm not sure Jousse would approve of this. He only talked about groups of twos and threes. But sometimes, it seems to me that a line really "introduces" a triplet:

And someone says, in a rising tone,
    "I'm saying something that rises even further,"
        And only now does the tension begin to fall,
        And this fourth line completes it.

You May Find Better Rhythms

So what rules have I used to break up these verses into groups? Here's my secret method: whatever sounds good.

There *isn't* any secret method. If you find a better rhythm for a cluster of verses, change it! And let me know! (bill@howtoremember.biz) I'd love to improve future editions.

Skip the Verse Numbers and Headings

You'll notice that, just now, when I showed you the rhythmic verse, I didn't include the verse numbers or any headings, such as "Pilate Condemns Jesus". Although that information is helpful, I do *not* think you should memorize it. For me, it's enough to know which book and chapter I'm memorizing from.

As you saw when you read Mark 15 earlier, I do include headings and some verse numbers in the full selection. But I don't suggest memorizing them.

If you wanted to know the chapter and verse, the best way would be to *say* "Mark, chapter fifteen, verse one" before that verse. But even if you shortened this to "Mark fifteen one," it would sound ridiculous, like a computer printout. It would disrupt the story, and kill the rhythm.

Expression (These Words Are *Alive*)

At first, speaking the Bible with rhythm may seem unnatural. Even disrespectful.

Why? Because we in the English-speaking world have this bizarre tradition of the **reverential monotone**.

Ditch the "Reverential Monotone"

Think about church. Unless you're very lucky, your lector "proclaims" the readings with less expression than your GPS. You'd get more drama from R2D2.

Somehow, we've gotten the idea that the Bible needs a *special* voice: a *dead monotone*.

But what's so reverent about a monotone? These words are alive, and so are you. A Bible is just a sacred suitcase to carry those words from Christ to you.

Sadly, the words had to have all the expression and intonation hacked off so they'd fit in the suitcase. Your job is to unpack them, and try to get them back to normal.

The monotone is not normal. The monotone is dead. When our cultural air is thick with the conviction that the Bible is a dead old distant book with nothing to offer, a monotone is the worst possible choice.

The monotone is also the worst possible choice for remembering.

Let the Words Live

Freeing the rhythms helps the words live. But you want to go even farther. You want to **tell the story**.

Think about telling a story to a friend. Or reading a story to a child. The expression comes naturally. It flows from what's happening in the story.

Tell the story. Expression will come naturally.

Now Speak Your Verse

That's all you need to get started! This has been a long first lesson, but don't worry. Soon you'll be focused on learning verses, not learning *how* to learn them.

Read the verses out loud:

- **loudly** and **slowly**

- with **rhythm** and **expression**

Throughout the rest of the day (or tomorrow, if it's already bedtime), **read the first verse out loud again every few hours**. Don't worry about memorizing it yet. Focus on speaking it well.

Your Memorizing Plan

Now that you know how to **speak out** a verse, let's back up and look at our overall plan for memorizing. Many people offer different methods for memorizing Scripture. I want you to understand why my *Books by Heart* approach is simple, easy, and natural.

A Daily Verse

The core idea is simple: every day, you learn one new verse, and repeat the verses you've already learned.

Learning one new verse every day, and renewing what you've learned, doesn't take long. We're talking **fifteen minutes** or so, spread throughout the day.

It may not seem like much. But this small effort gives you powerful leverage. The words of the Gospel are potent. They're like strong magnets, attracting thoughts and feelings that would otherwise rush by. Bit by bit, you will think differently.

Besides, the verses add up fast. By Holy Saturday, you'll know all of Good Friday, from Christ's interview with Pilate to the stone rolled across the door of the sepulchre.

Why Only One Verse a Day?

You may assume that memorizing is difficult. Or, you may be surprised that you're only learning one verse a day. Can't you do more?

Eventually, yes. But if this is your first time, you're training a new skill. Your mind is *extremely* susceptible to the patterns you set right from the beginning. If you tried to start out memorizing two or five or ten verses a day, you would inevitably start to rush, and then feel burdened and overwhelmed. The whole experience would sour.

Instead, focus on getting this one verse *right*. It's like push-ups. Ten push-ups with correct form will do much more for your body than twenty sloppy attempts.

Also, memorizing requires *review*. By only adding one new verse a day, your daily renewal won't take too long.

When you complete this project, if you want to learn more, you can try learning two new verses a day for a month. And then three. And so on.

But for now, stick to one. Master the art.

Why You *Can* Memorize

Maybe you're wondering whether you can *really* memorize even one new verse a day. Perhaps you're constantly reminded of your "bad memory" as your car keys vanish and critical mail evaporates.

Guess what? **I promise that your memory is *excellent*.** How do I know? **Because you can read.**

Think about it. If your memory were actually *broken*, would you be decoding these squiggles into words, linking them to *sounds*, snapping them into phrases and sentences, making the impossible leap into kaleidoscopes of *meaning* — all at hundreds of words per minute?

I don't care if you take reading for granted. I don't care how they graded you in school. You can read. Your memory is amazing. Period.

Whatever "memory" problems you have are due to *technique* and *habit*. These are precisely the skills you'll learn to improve in this book.

Even the most amazing tool will fail if you don't know how to use it. You're going to learn *how* to remember these verses.

Your Daily Routine

You'll only need to spend about **fifteen minutes a day** on this project.

Even better, you'll spread this time in bits throughout the day. Every day, you will:

- Repeat the verses you've already learned, all together, as a **series of stories**.

- **Learn** your **new verse**.

- Throughout the day, **repeat** your **new** verse **three or four times**.

- If you're having trouble with any older verses, repeat these too. You'll be surprised at how easily you can fit these short reviews into the crevices of your day.

- At the end of the day, **repeat all** your verses again **once**, including your new verse.

You might prefer to learn new material at the *end* of the day, sleep on it, then review throughout the next day. That's fine.

This daily routine is the core of learning by heart.

If you miss a day, pick up where you left off.

At the risk of making your Lent even harder (again), let's talk more about cookies.

We'll explore this routine in more detail later. This is all you need to get started.

Stories, Not Memory Tricks

I keep saying "verses", but the Gospels are a series of **stories**. Stories are much easier to think about and remember than individual verses.

If you've used other memory books, you know there's a wide variety of memory tricks out there. I've tried most of them. Sadly, much of this advice actually makes **memorizing verses more difficult**.

If this book saves you from even one standard mistake, it will pay for itself many times over.

For instance, have you heard about "mnemonics" or "memory palaces"? Some books suggest using these visual memory tricks for anything you want to learn, but I disagree.

For this project, **you don't need any wacky memory tricks**. You won't need to imagine any crazy pictures or funky memory sentences.

Instead, you'll learn how to make the **verses themselves** a **memorable experience**. You'll unlock their power with **rhythm**, **expression**, and **imagination**.

Mnemonics aren't inherently harmful. If you want to memorize your credit card number, mnemonics work great. But they're not the right tool for memorizing texts. I'll explain why further on.

For now, let's move to the next step in memorizing. As you speak a verse out, you also **take the verse in**.

Take the Verses In

You've learned how to **speak the verses out**:

- Speak **loudly** and **slowly**

- With **rhythm** and **expression**

Now you'll learn how to take verses *in* as you speak them.

When you **take verses in**, you:

- **See** the words and phrases

- **Hear** the words and phrases

- **Feel** the **rhythms**

- **Feel** the **shapes** of the words on your **tongue**

See the Words

The first step to taking in the verse is to see the words. This seems obvious. But when I say *see*, I mean *intense attention*.

Reading this book, you've already seen and understood thousands of words. But *how* have you seen them? Right now, close your eyes, count to ten, and try to call up images of these pages.

What did you see? Anything? At best, you probably got a fleeting glimpse or two.

Does this mean you have a "bad" memory? No. Your mind did exactly what you've trained it to do.

It slurped the *meaning* from the words as quickly as possible. Why didn't you keep mental snapshots of every page, like Sherlock Holmes, Monk, or Shawn Spencer?

For the same reason you didn't keep the can the last time you opened some tuna. You didn't need to. Your mind has better things to do than hold onto every page you read, and it knows it.

But now it's time to take those mental snapshots. You want to train your mind to "photograph" each verse.

That may sound impossible. But think of all the pristine mental images you *can* call up. (Corporate logo trivia, anyone?) Learning to capture verses simply takes practice and good technique.

"Photographing" Each Verse

Intend to see perfectly. Tell yourself that you can and will remember this verse exactly as you see it on the page or screen.

Look with intense **attention**. Normally, your gaze races down sentences. Instead, look as if you were looking at a painting. See these words as a unique visual image, not mere symbols.

Focus on **details**. Don't try to "photograph" the entire verse at once. Study it phrase by phrase. Notice the font, the spacing, the place on the page. All these little details seem to come together in our minds like the tiles of a mosaic.

As you try to recall the verse later, **refresh** your memory as needed. If you forget something, look at the verse again. Fill in the gaps.

Over your first few recitations, you'll remember some bits, but not others. Make the effort to remember. But if you don't get it after a few seconds, look at the book. There's no point in waiting. Get those missing mosaic tiles. Your goal is an *effortless* memory.

True, if you check too quickly, you may train yourself to always need the book. You may even trick yourself into thinking you can't memorize at all. But this is a balance you'll have to work out for yourself. Even if you only remember one or two more words each time, you're moving in the right direction.

Be patient with yourself. This may be a brand new skill for you. If you have to keep checking, don't worry. Gradually, you'll learn how to see clearly.

Perfection Is Easier Than "Almost"

Should you try to learn the verses *perfectly*? Yes. Because perfection is easier than "almost".

I know this because I have "almost" memorized hundreds of verses. I've memorized the entire Gospel of Mark — *almost*. When I learned this Gospel, I was using a different system, so I didn't learn them perfectly. Today, I can say many verses perfectly. But I'll say many verses with a slight paraphrase, or the occasional missed word or phrase.

You might think, so what? What's a mistake here and there, if you still basically know the whole Gospel?

For years, I thought so too. Then I realized something. Every time I hit a patch I wasn't perfectly sure about, I had to *hesitate*. I had to consider two or more possibilities for what came next.

Not only did this waste time and cause anxiety, but it made the whole memory *shakier*. Blurrier. More likely to fail next time.

These days, I'm "polishing" my Mark memories. I know that whenever I hit a verse where I'm uncertain, I need to check the text and repair this memory right away. When I skip this, I make more work for myself. My mind knows that I'm not sure about this verse. Next time, my hesitation will be the same, or worse.

Instead, I need to check the text and make that repair. *Now.*

You Remember That You Forget

Back when I was settling for "almost", I was actually memorizing the *entire experience* of not quite knowing the verse.

Your memory is that amazing. You can memorize that you have trouble memorizing something.

The stronger this flawed memory becomes, the harder it becomes to ever learn the verse correctly. You have too much mental baggage, half-memories of all the different versions you concocted in your mental thrashing. It's a mess.

By contrast, when you know a verse perfectly, you *know* you know it perfectly. It's easy. No more stress. You get a flash of exactly how the verse looks or sounds.

It's easier to learn a verse perfectly than to almost learn it. The key is to correct your uncertainties right away by checking the book.

The Context of the Story

Many books and websites offer a "daily verse," isolated from anything else. In the first edition of *Christmas by Heart*, I did the same thing myself, and showed each day's verse on its own page. They looked so nice, with all that lovely white space.

But you won't get good results if you try to memorize a verse all alone on a page. Instead, read and reread each verse in its place in the full story. Seeing the verse as part of the story, rather than alone on a page, puts the verse into **context**. As you read and reread each verse, this unique context will help you remember.

Hear the Words

Just as important as *seeing* each verse is to **hear the words**. As I said earlier, you should always hear yourself saying these words.

You should physically **hear yourself** saying these verses.

When you say verses out loud, you're literally talking to yourself.

We "talk to ourselves" all the time, but most of this conversation happens inside our heads. For memorizing, that isn't enough. You want to hear your own voice.

Hearing activates more parts of your mind and memory than the usual mental self-talk. Remember, the more ways you connect to these verses, the better you'll remember them.

Feel the Rhythms

We've already talked about speaking the **rhythms in the Bible**. These rhythms can change your whole experience of these stories.

But the rhythms go beyond speaking. When you speak with rhythm, you also *hear* rhythm. You even *feel* it. You can *feel* the pause, the tension, the resolution.

You don't need constant awareness of these rhythms. Mostly, you sense them without realizing it. But sometimes, especially when you're starting a new verse, or the passage is difficult, you can help clarify the memory by paying attention to the feel of the rhythm.

Feel the Shapes of the Words in Your Tongue and Mouth

You can also **feel the shapes of the words** in your tongue and mouth.

Try it. Go to the full story at the back of the book, and read yesterday's and today's verses together three times.

- First, as you would normally read aloud.

- Second, as you learned to speak earlier: **loudly** and **slowly**, with **rhythm** and **expression**.

- Third, paying attention to **forming each word** with your **tongue, lips, and mouth.**

Did you feel the difference?

When you feel the shapes of the words, you get **clarity**. It's like a muffled voice becoming clear.

As with feeling the rhythms, you don't need to be constantly aware of these sensations. But they're another layer of experiencing these words. If you give some attention to shaping the words, especially when you're first learning verses, it can help etch the words into your mind.

These shapes help make words and phrases *unique*. The more unique they are, the better your mind can remember them.

Renew Your Verses

As you learn more about memorizing, remember that **daily renewal is core of learning**.

> Repeat your new verse three or four times today.
>
> At the end of the day (or tomorrow morning), repeat all the verses you've learned as a series of stories.

Remember, focus on **speaking each verse out** ...

- Speak **loudly** and **slowly**

- With **rhythm** and **expression**

... and **taking each verse in** ...

- **See** the words and phrases

- **Hear** the words and phrases

- **Feel** the **rhythms**

- **Feel** the **shapes** of the words on your **tongue**

Try to say these verses without looking at the book. But if you get stuck, reread them. Remembering should *never* be a struggle.

Learning these verses should not be a self-test! We're doing the exact **opposite of a test**. On a test, you're punished for finding the right answer outside yourself. Here in real life, what matters is *knowing*. If your memory isn't clear yet, read the book and clarify it. Once you make clear memories, remembering will be almost effortless.

Experience

So far, you've learned how to **speak the verses out**:

- Speak **loudly** and **slowly**
- With **rhythm** and **expression**

And also how to **take the verses in**:

- **See** the words and phrases
- **Hear** the words and phrases
- **Feel** the **rhythms**
- **Feel** the **shapes** of the words on your **tongue**

Now you'll learn how to **experience the verses** in your **thoughts** and **imagination**.

Move Through the Words into Thoughts

Imagining is both the simplest and the most mysterious aspect of learning these stories by heart.

It's simple because, in theory, we all know how to imagine. At the very least, we dream every night.

But the mystery of imagination sometimes bewilders me. Imagination is so *personal*. We hardly have the language to articulate what happens inside our heads.

The obvious meaning for "imagination" is a mental *image*, like a picture or movie. But what we do with these verses can be much more complex.

Here's the critical point: you want to **move through** the **words** into **thoughts**.

Move through the words into thoughts.

These thoughts can include:

- scenes and sensations

- places

- feelings

- memories

- meaning

Scenes and Sensations

Obviously, whenever you can, you want to imagine the *scene*. What's happening?

You can see images and hear sounds, like you're watching a movie. But use your other senses too. Taste. Smell. Touch.

You can experience *any sensation* you can remember. We hear songs "in our head", but you can also smell the stink of the crowd in Pilate's courtyard, and feel the splintery chafe of the cross.

Places

Think of your sense of *space*, of a place opening around you. Your imagination, like the real world, is three-dimensional.

When you use your sense of space, you can put yourself *into* the scene. You can experience it as if it's happening to you.

When Pilate argues with Jesus, don't just see a tiny Station of the Cross plaque. *Look around.* Even if you're in your bedroom, you can *be* in the marble hall of the palace, damp and chilly with the morning air, and hear the crowd rumbling outside.

Or, you can ground your scenes in actual places that you know. Even been to court for a ticket? Sit on one of those benches. Put Christ in an orange jump-suit, handcuffed, in line with a drug addict and a rapist. He stands at a table in front, and all you can see is his back, while a stern but kindly old judge tries to talk some sense into him.

Feelings

How does the scene make you feel? What about the people in the scene? Can you feel what they're going through? Emotions can shock you with their intensity.

Memories

Think about your life memories. Has anything like this ever happened to you? Linking to a scene from your own life creates a powerful resonance.

Meaning

Not every verse describes a scene you can visualize. That's fine. Abstract thought is important too. A verse can inspire a whole train of thought.

Some memory guides place a huge emphasis on visual memory, and I did so myself when I was starting out. I needed this emphasis. I found out my visual imagination was incredibly more powerful than I'd assumed.

But not *all* thinking has to be visual.

This list of possible thoughts only scratches the surface. You can think about these verses in as many ways as you can think.

Imagining Is a New Skill

The problem? Thinking takes work. For most of us, imagining is a new skill, and that means effort.

Our default response to reading is the easy route
— identification. Identification is the great hazard of
memorizing.

We read that first verse:

And straightway in the morning,
    the chief priests holding a consultation
with the ancients and the scribes
    and the whole council,
binding Jesus,
    led him away
        and delivered him to Pilate.

And we think, "Oh, right, the chief priests. I
know who they are. And Jesus. And Pontius Pilate.
And morning. Identified. Done. What's next? I've
heard this story *so many times*."

This ordinary reading happens on a superficial
level. We don't *imagine* anything. We don't *think*
much at all, unless something happens to strike us.

And that's fine. Ordinary reading is quite useful
for ordinary purposes.

Ordinary reading is like walking through the forest. You don't need to be aware of the unique con-
tours of every tree. You just need to keep an eye out
for berries (and bears).

Our minds are fantastically equipped to be constantly awash in seas of information, and attract only
the essential bits. We excel at this. If we didn't, we
would starve to death trying to make breakfast.

Most of what you read doesn't matter. Your mind
plucks the essentials, and forgets the rest.

Now, however, you're suddenly asking your mind to remember *every word*. This is a new skill.

You've become an aspiring artist. You've hauled your easel out into the forest, and you have to learn to *look*.

Like any new skill, deliberate imagining takes practice. You need to slow down and *think*. Branch out. What can these words lead you to? What can they *connect* to?

Imagining Is Connecting

Look again through that list of ways to think about the verses. Notice how they're all **connections**.

You imagine the cross by *connecting* this idea to the *sensations* of real logs. They're heavy, they scratch. They bite into your skin.

You imagine the *fear* and *pain* of Christ in the dock by *connecting* to your memories of your own emotions. We've all felt rejection. With a tiny bit of thought, those emotions flood back.

We often think of memorizing as a special, arcane skill. But memorizing, like imagining, is ultimately connecting. You think, "I want to tell the story of when Christ accepted death," and that concept *connects* both to the actual words of the story and to the vivid thoughts you've crafted.

Why do you forget things? Because you lose connections. The data doesn't get *erased*, as if you're a hard drive. The data gets *lost*. It sinks into the murky seas of your subconscious. That's why you can forget someone's name, but as soon as you hear it, *you remember it.* The name was in your head, but you couldn't find it.

This leads to a powerful idea. When you connect the words of the verses to vivid thoughts like scenes, places, memories, and feelings, those connections don't only help you experience the verses. They help you *remember* them.

Imagining is **connecting**.

Memorizing is also **connecting**.

What do you connect to? **Your own experiences.** You connect new material to what you already know.

Imagining Brings Delight

Your own experiences are incredibly vivid. In fact, the word *vivid* comes from the Latin word for "life". Your experiences *are* your life. The more you connect verses to your own experience, the more you literally make them *come to life*.

Let's take a simpler example. Read this sentence:

John ate a cookie.

Normally, this sentence would not detain us. "John" is probably a little boy. And we all know what eating a cookie is. This kind of filler clogs the arteries of many a mediocre bedtime story.

But suppose I actually walked into the room with a platter of cookies. Your *favorite* kind. Freshly baked.

In real life, there's nothing boring about a platter of fresh cookies. It doesn't matter that this incident isn't movie material. It doesn't matter that you've already eaten thousands of cookies over the course of your lifetime. When you *smell* your favorite kind of cookie, and take that bite ... life is good.

Now here's the crazy part. As you read this, is your mouth actually watering? In a way, you just *did* eat a cookie.

I know this isn't *The Matrix*. I'm not trying to blur the crucial distinction between imagination and real life. I am trying to show you how closely they intertwine. Your real life is far more *available* to you, as memories, than you realize.

You can sit here and experience eating your favorite kind of cookie. You can *relive* the smell, the taste, the warmth, the feel of the food in your fingers and your mouth.

(Maybe I should have eaten breakfast before I wrote this lesson.)

I keep saying "your favorite kind," because that helps point you to *specific* experiences. We don't sit down and eat the Platonic ideal of a cookie, like that poorly drawn character in the children's book. We eat an oatmeal cookie, or a chocolate chip cookie, or a banana nut cookie, or a peanut butter cookie, or a gingerbread cookie, or a molasses cookie ... they are each *different*. Unique. Precious.

You can only remember eating a *specific* kind of cookie. If you don't know which cookie you're eating, you're still thinking abstract thoughts *about* eating cookies. You're not smelling any warm cinnamon or tasting any peanut butter.

If you do succeed in remembering actual tastes and smells — you'll know! It's a *jolt*. You will *feel* these things again. It's so different from abstract thought.

I'm afraid we need to wrap up this cookie meditation. (I hope this reflection hasn't unduly exacerbated one of your Lenten sacrifices.)

But here's the takeaway. If you wanted to, you could relive all these delightful memories as soon as you read:

> John ate a cookie.

That one sentence could be enough.

"Unpacking" the Cookie

And you could go even further, beyond this sugar-free approach to enjoying dessert.

If you have small children or grandchildren, you could remember how they look when you give them a dessert, how happy you are to make them happy.

You could think about how children enjoy food, with no fear or guilt. On the other hand, you could consider how this innocence has led to an epidemic of childhood obesity and diabetes.

You could find yourself musing on the balance between enjoyment and temperance, on the search for delight that does no harm … suddenly John is exploring a forest, making a snowman, feasting on grapes in the middle of winter …

I'll stop my cookie exegesis. But sometimes I think I've found the secret to why so much language in Scripture, and the texts and stories from other ancient cultures, are so sparse and succinct. They had no TVs. No one did their imagining for them.

They didn't need painstaking descriptions and telling details before they slowly began to imagine a mob. You just said, "and when the multitude came up," and their minds exploded into cinematic fireworks.

I can't prove this, of course. But I'm fairly sure.

And the delights of imagination are entirely unique. They are *creative*. What is creativity, anyway, but making new connections?

Move beyond **identification** to **connect** with your **experiences**. These connections can bring intense, creative **delight**.

Your New Daily Routine

Over the last few lessons, you've learned the essential skills you'll need to remember these verses.

- **Speak out**: Speak **loudly** and **slowly**, with **rhythm** and **expression**.

- **Take it in**: As you speak, **see** the words as they are written, **hear** the words you say, and **feel** the **rhythms** and the **shapes** of the words on your tongue.

- **Experience**: Let the words lead you to **imagine the scene** in this **story**.

You've also begun to memorize new verses. And you're renewing what you learn, using the **daily routine** I showed you earlier.

Now I'd like to explore that routine further. Why does it work? How can you fit this time easily into your schedule, and remember to do it?

Spaced Repetition and "Smart" Intervals

If we were going to memorize a longer text, such as an entire Gospel, I would teach you about "spaced repetition" and "smart intervals". In spaced repetition, you take advantage of how the brain functions to time your reviews as efficiently as possible.

The basic idea is simple. At the *beginning*, when you first learn material, you have to repeat it many times. This repetition seems to convince the brain that, unlike the rest of the torrent of information engulfing you each day, this material is worth holding onto.

After these early repetitions, you slowly leave more and more space between your repetitions. Before long, you're waiting weeks, months, and years between repetitions.

You can use free computer flashcard programs like Anki to track each bit of material automatically. This brilliant system of "spaced repetition" can help you retain huge amounts of material in your mind.

A Simpler Method: Repeat Every Day

However, spaced repetition also requires a certain amount of planning. I'll explain that method in upcoming books which involve memorizing more material. For the stories in this book, the overhead isn't worth it.

Instead, let's keep things simple. Every day, at least twice, recite all the verses you've learned so far. Say them together, as a series of stories.

Every day, at least twice, recite all the verses you've learned so far. Say them together, as a series of stories.

You won't have to do this forever. For now, since we're "only" learning about a chapter's worth of verses, it's easy and quick to just recite it all every day during Lent.

At the end of the book, I'll explain how you can maintain these verses into the future, without having to say them every day.

Say Recent Verses More Often If Needed

Ideally, twice a day will be enough for all the verses you've already learned. But you may find that you're uncertain about one or more verses, especially the verses you only learned yesterday or the day before.

No problem. At the start of the day, when you say all the verses you've learned, pay attention to when you hit your first uncertain verse.

Normally, the next step would be to learn your new verse, and then repeat only that new verse an extra three or four times throughout the day.

But when you hit an uncertain verse, *start there* and recite up to and including your new verse throughout the day.

These extra recitations will only take a minute or two, but they'll make all the difference. Again, you start with the earliest "shaky" verse that you had trouble with, and recite through to today's new verse. Easy.

Strengthening Uncertain Verses

Let's say that you've learned from Mark 15, verses 1 to 6. Today, you plan to learn verse 7.

But when you start reciting from verse 1, you find that you're unsure about verse 4.

You learn verse 7, as planned. Then, throughout the day, you recite verses 4 through 7 (not just your new verse 7), three or four times.

In the evening, you recite the whole thing again, from verse 1 up through verse 7.

Your Daily Verse Routine

Once more, here's the full daily routine:

- First, in the morning, say all the verses you've already learned.

- If any verses are uncertain, refresh your memory from the book. Note the earliest uncertain verse that you have trouble with.

- Then, study today's new verse. Repeat the new verse several times as you learn it.

- Every few hours, start with the earliest uncertain verse, and recite straight through to your new verse. Do this **three or four times** altogether.

- Later in the day, say all the verses again. (They make a perfect extra bedtime story.)

Crafting Your Routine

Learning these verses depends on **daily time**. It doesn't take much time, but it does need to be done every day. You face two obstacles:

- Finding time to say the verses

- Making it a habit (actually saying them)

Finding Time to Recite

Can you say these verses while you're doing something else? That's the first place to look, because you won't even have to change your schedule.

Do you already take a walk every day? Or have a time when you read and relax? Or put your kids to bed? How about morning or evening prayer?

Learning and reciting verses won't merely "fit" into these slots. These new habits improve them.

For instance, prayer. With a little thought, learning and reciting verses can easily become a prayer.

Bedtime Stories

If you have kids, get ready for major synergy.

When I put my kids to bed, I read them their bedtime stories, and then I say some verses. If I had *replaced* the stories with verses, there might have been a mutiny. But they're perfectly happy to get the verses as *extra* stories.

By now, if I don't say verses, they're disappointed. Even better, they've learned huge chunks of my verses just by *listening*. When I hesitate, they sometimes pipe right up.

In fact, they often want to interrupt and ask questions. We can wind up launching into a mini-seminar. If I tried to *schedule* "Bible discussion time" during the day, I could easily waste a lot of effort trying to pry out some interest. But because it's bedtime, and because when Papa leaves, that's it for the day, suddenly all this Scriptural interest blossoms unbidden. Sometimes I have to ask them to stop interrupting.

You're going to tell these stories anyway, for your own practice. With a little planning, you can make your storytelling enrich your family's lives.

Making a Habit

Habit is crucial. You've probably heard that it takes around **three weeks** to form a new habit.

Hook to Your Existing Habits

The easiest way to start a new habit is to **hook it to something you already do every day.** For instance:

- Getting up and going to bed

- Breakfast, lunch, and dinner

- Morning and/or evening prayer

- Putting the kids to bed

Can you say these verses when you first get up, and right before you go to bed? How about before or after a meal? If you already pray every day, definitely consider including a recitation.

A Simple Daily Routine

- When you wake up, say all your verses, and learn your new verse.

- Before or after each meal, start at your earliest uncertain verse, and recite up through your new verse.

- In the evening, after your prayers (or reading a bedtime story), say all your verses.

Get Someone to Pester You

You should also get someone to pester you. The grownup word for this is "accountability". But Jesus didn't tell any parables about "accountability." He did tell a parable about a widow driving an unjust judge crazy.

In my case the kids take care of this. "Do you have any verses tonight, Papa?" they ask, in that special kid voice that is hopeful, hesitant, and (sometimes) infuriatingly irresistible.

Track Your Progress Like Seinfeld

Remember Jerry Seinfeld? Supposedly, an aspiring comedian once asked him the secret to success. According to the story, Seinfeld told him that:

- A comedian needs to be as funny as possible.

- The only way to get funnier is to practice writing jokes.

- So you need to write jokes **every day**.

- And the best way to make sure you do this every day is a **huge chart on your wall**, with a **year's worth of daily boxes**.

- Every day, if you write your jokes, you put an "X" in the box.

- Pretty soon, you have a chain of X's.

Success, according to Seinfeld, is simple. "Don't break the chain!"

I've tried this "Seinfeld chart," and let me tell you, it's the most effective habit-building tool I've ever seen.

From where I write, I can glance over and *see* my charts, one for each habit I'm trying to form or maintain. (For instance, writing this book.) Look at all those X's! Pow! Instant affirmation doesn't get any sweeter. All those X's are things I've actually *done*, not goals or "To Do" items.

So use a chart. No excuses. I've made a free chart for you at **LentByHeart.com**. Download it, print it off, and tape it somewhere prominent. Put a marker, preferably bright red, within arm's reach of where you hang it. Not a pencil. You want to see these marks from across the room.

And don't just use that parish monthly calendar you get for free. It's critical to see *several months* at once.

Daily Recitation Times + Chart = Habit

We've boiled this new habit down into two steps:

Step 1: Plan precisely when you're going to say your verses each day. Don't bother about *times*. Focus on *hooks*. Which daily habits will you hook your verses to?

Step 2: Go to **LentByHeart.com**. Print the daily "Seinfeld chart". (Disclaimer: No, this chart is not officially endorsed by or associated with Seinfeld in any way.) Tape the chart to the wall in a place where you can easily see and mark it.

With your daily routine planned, and a chart to track your progress, you'll soon find you have a habit.

Bible Stories

In the last lesson, you learned how to craft your personal **daily routine** for saying verses. Have you tried hooking your recitations to any habits yet? If any of your decisions didn't work, don't worry. Today's a new day. Try again, or try something else. You can always tweak.

Gospels as Stories

We're used to dividing the Bible into chapters and verses. But nobody applied this system to the Gospels until centuries after they were written. When people first heard Mark, they heard a series of *stories*.

Today, **biblical storytellers** have brought back this focus on the Gospels as stories. Scholars such as David Rhoads and Tom Boomershine have written books with titles like *Mark As Story* and *Story Journey*. There's even a Network of Biblical Storytellers.

When they meet, the festivities include tellings of whole books of the Bible.

Jousse taught me to find the Bible rhythms. These folks taught me to find the Bible stories. When I first started memorizing Scripture, I still focused on chapters and verses. Now I understand that the earlier unit of *story* is far more natural, memorable, and enjoyable.

The word "story" here is broader than what we usually mean (a tale with a protagonist and a beginning, middle, and end). In this context, a "story" is basically a series of verses that hang naturally together. It could be the conversation between Jesus and Nicodemus in the third chapter of John, or the first section of the Sermon on the Mount.

Remembering Stories

How do you divide verses into stories? There are no hard and fast rules.

For Mark 15, I have three major stories:

- Condemned by Pilate

- Crucifixion

- Burial

Our basic unit of learning the Gospels isn't the verse, but the **story**. You're learning the **stories** of the Passion.

You could break these into smaller "stories", if you liked. I've included small story headings where I would make these breaks.

But for our purposes, the story divisions don't really matter. We're repeating the whole thing each day. Story breaks are useful with a larger amount of material, because you can recite particular *stories* each day, rather than everything you've ever learned.

In the future, as you learn other texts, you can also recite entire chapters. Many chapters seem to break between stories.

You might think that single verses are easier to remember than whole stories. Verses are so much shorter! If you only wanted to remember one verse, this would be true. But since you're learning many verses, you'll find that they naturally snap together into stories.

Reciting in Different Ways

By now, you've recited these verses in different ways.

You've **read** them slowly, learning them for the first time, and using all the methods for speaking out, taking in, and imagining.

You've **reread** them, as you filled in the gaps of your memory.

You've gradually tried to **say them without looking**. When you've come to a tough patch, you've checked the words, to solidify your memory.

Sometimes I call this check a "rinse". At this stage, it feels like I'm slowly washing away the mud of my muddled forgetting, getting to the crystal clear memory beneath.

If you've been speaking the verses to friends or family members, you're already **telling the verses as stories**. No matter how much expression you use by yourself, speaking to others can bring out more. If you haven't told the verses to anyone yet, try it!

Or at least plan on trying it when you feel you've learned enough verses to tell a complete story.

Can you say the first few verses perfectly? If so, try a new way to recite them: **fast**. I've read more than one memorizer recommend that you say the words as quickly as you can.

Why fast? For one thing, it's different. Remember, different methods help strengthen your memories.

In my case, I find that speed can clear away some unnecessary hesitations. The extra effort helps me focus. I know these verses better than I think I do.

I used to think that a fast recitation was incompatible with imagining. Actually, no matter how fast you can talk, you can imagine faster.

But you have to be careful about speaking fast. You don't want to slip into a mindset of *rushing*, where you're trying to minimize your verse time as a "necessary evil."

Rushing, in fact, is the bane of happy learning.

Renewing Is Its Own Reward

It's extremely tempting to rush through recitations. But when we **rush**, we **defeat the whole purpose** of learning verses in the first place.

Rushing through your verses defeats the whole point of learning them.

Renewing the verses is its own reward.

Think about it. Why did you decide to learn the story of the Passion?

It's not a rhetorical question. Only you can say.

I do know that your goal includes knowing these verses by heart. But this actually gets rather complex. You want to *know* these verses so you can *think* with them, right? This can't just be a checkbox on a list of a thousand things to do before you die. You want to weave these words into your mind, so that your mind will move in *new thoughts*, thoughts you'd otherwise never have.

You may have other goals, too, like sharing the verses with your children or congregation. But whether you're interested in study or prayer (or both), I'm almost certain that you're hoping to *think differently* than you did before you started.

Here's the surprise. *You're already thinking differently.* Every time you renew these verses, *you're thinking about them.*

These new thoughts are not some distant goal that can only come when you've done the gruntwork of learning the verses. No. You've already arrived — as long as you don't rush.

Baking Cookies vs. Riding a Bike

This feels too abstract. Time to get concrete. At the risk of making your Lent even harder (again), let's talk more about cookies.

Think about making cookies. You do a whole bunch of weird rituals — breaking eggs, measuring pulverized grains, mixing in distilled herbs. You spread this gooey concoction onto a metal plate, and you put it into an oven. It's all quite bizarre. But at the end, if the magic works, you get to eat cookies.

Eating cookies is *nothing* like *baking* cookies. The two processes differ entirely. Most of us enjoy eating cookies. Enjoying the baking? That's an acquired taste. Some of us *endure* baking, for the sake of the cookies at the end.

Many goals in life share this same dynamic. If you want cookies, you have to bake them. If you want a house, you have to build it. If you want money, you have to work for it.

If you're lucky, you hunt for work you'll enjoy. But the work is still different from the mysterious magic of money.

This dynamic of work-then-reward gets burned into our brain. But not everything is like this

Think about riding a bike. When you first get onto a bike, you wobble and struggle and probably fall. But even so, you roll a few feet. You are practicing the *same* process that you hope to achieve.

One day, you'll ride so well that these early attempts will feel like another lifetime. And yet, you're *already biking*.

You can see this with kids. They don't say, "I want to go practice riding my bike, so that one day I can actually ride my bike." They want to *ride their bikes*, as well as they can, right now.

You're Already Thinking

If you're like me, you were first drawn to memorization as an exotic, foreign skill. You thought it would be like baking cookies. You would do all these arcane tricks, and then — ta-da! — you would relish the completely unrelated result.

But verses are like riding a bike. You're *already* thinking.

All the methods I'm showing you — Bible rhythms, daily renewal, imagining — they're simply different ways to *think* about these verses.

They aren't like baking, where you're not even supposed to taste the batter. No, you're already on the bike, already moving, already thinking.

You may have started out with a focus on *memorizing*, on the magic of getting the words perfect. That's still a worthy goal.

But memorizing is the *fruit* of thinking. Not the other way around.

Don't Waste Time "Memorizing"

I wasted a lot of time (a *lot*) trying to memorize things as "efficiently" as I could. I assumed that I wouldn't really think about the verses until after I'd memorized them.

This is precisely backwards. You start thinking about the verses right away, as soon as you read them. That's why we have books, to help us think. And you wean yourself off the training wheels of the book *by thinking*. You use these methods to *help you think* about the verses you've read.

Yes, it's grand when you can think so well that you no longer need the book. But this work depends entirely on the *quality of your thoughts*. You're not a hard drive. You're a thinker.

Don't think you need to "memorize" these verses first before you begin to enjoy new and exciting thoughts. **You're already thinking.**

Renewing Is Its Own Reward

I've talked about memorizing "efficiently". I used to think that "efficiency" meant "getting it over with as soon as possible."

Now I understand that, in memorization, "efficiency" means focusing on the methods that *help you think*.

Why does everyone hate rote repetition? Because it doesn't engage your thoughts. It feels like slave labor. You repeat words until you can't stand them any more. A few months later, if you don't renew them, you forget them anyway.

True, our time is limited. We have other responsibilities and desires besides learning the story of the Passion by heart. It is sensible to find "efficient" ways to memorize.

But when we use these methods, when we come to those times for saying verses, we need to *enter that time* as its *own reward*.

Learning these verses means that you have special times throughout the day when you think about Christ. Enjoy them.

Don't Watch the Clock

Most of the skills I'm teaching you are straightforward. You can learn to follow a sequence of simple steps.

But imagination is open-ended. One verse may instantly transport you to a vivid scene. With another, you may have to mull over it for several minutes.

I know I said that you only need to spend about fifteen minutes a day on this. But don't watch the clock. If you take an extra five or ten minutes to imagine well, good for you! Don't rush!

Rushing Wastes Time

If we *rush*, we're telling ourselves that this is just gruntwork. We're saying that we're not really doing anything worthwhile. We feel that we're simply paying in installments for a car we'll eventually get to drive.

This is sad. Instead of enjoying the time, instead of savoring the delights of imagination, we're snapping on our own shackles. We're making a little more of our day into dead, grumpy, time.

Even worse, we're also *messing up our memorization*. Rushing simply *doesn't work*.

Memorizing is a *complete experience*. You're connecting, remember? These verses will connect to *everything* that's happening to you while you think about them — including your emotions. If you always resent the time you spend on verses ... how much do you expect your mind to enjoy revisiting these memories? How strong do you think these memories will be?

"Saving time" by rushing only wastes all of it.

Renewing rewards you.

Rushing wastes your time.

Renew, Don't Review

Have you noticed that I try to say "renew" instead of "review"? Switching these words has been a paradigm shift for me.

"Review" conjures up all the worst parts of school:

- You're forced to do it. It's a chore.

- You review for the sake of some quiz or test, not the material itself.

- You're rehashing old stuff, in the same boring way.

But "renewing" feels totally different. We *renew* because we *want* to. You renew a friendship by calling up someone you love. You renew your strength every time you eat.

And renewing is *creative*. Another paradox: we memorize old words to lead us to new thoughts. Yes, we're also renewing the thoughts and connections we've already made. But you don't need to stop there. Renewing should be creative.

Renewing your memories is an act of *creativity*. You can think *new* thoughts every time you touch these verses.

Renewing is its own reward.

So don't hurry through renewal as one more task. Learn to savor your time with these verses.

A Beautiful, Old, Oral Translation

Learning to enjoy renewals can be a challenge. Here's another odd challenge to enjoy: the quirky old translation we're using. This old translation offers some surprising hidden features.

Why Use an Old Translation?

In case you haven't noticed, the translation you're memorizing is … old. "Thees" and "thous" are liberally sprinkled throughout sentences that feel rather Shakespearean.

The language sounds strange. The rhythms are different. Occasionally, a word is completely foreign.

The reasons are simple. This is the Douay-Rheims Challoner translation. It was originally composed in the sixteenth and seventeenth centuries, then heavily revised in the eighteenth century. That's old. To our modern ears, the DRC is extremely similar to the more well-known King James Bible, also from the seventeenth century.

Almost every church you could attend will read a more modern translation. Why do I use this version?

Freedom

First, because this version is in the public domain.

I don't see the point of memorizing anything under copyright, at least not if you have a free option. We memorize to *recreate*. Copyright shackles this creativity.

True, you probably wouldn't get sued for repeating a copyrighted translation to your children. But freedom matters, and it begins in theory.

Almost all contemporary translations of the Bible are under copyright. Open any devotional book, and the small print will include a note explaining that the Bible verses are quoted with permission.

I appreciate the tremendous effort and expense that goes into translation. This is not the place to tackle the logistics of both claiming a text is Divine Revelation and then putting it under copyright. It's complicated.

Fortunately, a translation in the public domain neatly sidesteps all this. The public domain is free.

Oral Rhythms

The DRC also offers a surprise side benefit: **oral rhythms**.

In his major work *Orality and Literacy*, Walter J. Ong compares a passage from the Douay Old Testament (the seventeenth century version) to the same passage from the contemporary *New American Bible*.

We might think the Douay is different simply because it's "old". But Ong shows that the Douay is *oral*, "produced in a culture with a still massive oral residue."

This is huge.

Bible rhythms are critical to moving *beyond* reading, into *speaking* these verses. This quaint, arcane translation of the DRC is actually *better suited* to oral recitation than almost all contemporary translations.

In my memorizing, I've found two main aspects of the DRC that, although they distracted me at first, turned out to be helpful oral features.

The Opening "And"

Did your teacher ever tell you not to begin a sentence with "And"? Have you noticed that practically *every other verse* you've learned so far from the DRC begins with "And"? Why the difference?

As Ong explains, the use of "And" is *oral*. Think about how you tell a story. You naturally say, "We did this. And then we did this. Oh, and then that happened." We use those *connecting* words in the rhythm of speech.

When we *write*, we feel we have to *edit out* that part of the natural speech rhythm. Modern Bible translations use all sorts of variations on the opening "And". But in the original Greek, all those sentences really do begin with a word similar to "And".

These modern translations are meant to be *read*, not *spoken* and *heard*. Pick up a modern Bible, and read the verses you've learned so far *out loud*. Now say your DRC verses. Can you hear how all those repetitions of "And" sound more like natural speech?

Repetition

This leads to a larger difference between oral and written culture: **repetition**. Your teacher probably also taught you not to keep repeating the same word. If your character is *sad* at the beginning of the paragraph, he can't be *sad* again for awhile. He has to be *wistful* or *depressed* or *downcast*. Out comes the thesaurus.

Even for writing, this advice is problematic. For speech, it's fatal. In speaking, repetition is *essential*. Think about good speeches, or even commercials. They always repeat the essential points. Commercials cram the company name as many times into thirty seconds as is humanly possible. They say the phone number at least twice, if not three or four times. *Repetition makes you remember.*

Repetition can also stir *emotion*. The same word acquires stronger and stronger meaning, building like a wave.

When you see words or phrases repeated in the DRC, try not to mentally filter them out. When you speak them, the repetition will help you remember, and help you feel the rhythms.

What About Accuracy?

Yes, biblical scholarship has advanced since the eighteenth century. The DRC has the special disadvantage of being a "translation of a translation," since it's based on the Latin Vulgate (although they did consult the original Hebrew and Greek texts). Some spots are certainly less accurate than a contemporary translation.

However, translation isn't an exact science. For the stories we're learning, the differences from contemporary translations are more a matter of language than actual "errors".

Besides, don't forget the oral rhythms. We may lose some textual accuracy with the DRC, but we also gain back some oral rhythms.

Arcane Language

Arcane language can help or hinder. In many passages, the old language has a force and beauty that seems lost in most modern translations.

In other places, the sentence construction, or even the vocabulary, is just too foreign for me. I find myself adjusting the phrasing, as the forces of mental gravity tug the phrases into shapes more consistent with my internal laws of linguistic physics.

But it's still worth the effort to learn the text perfectly. Unless you want to mark the text with your edits, so you can see them, you should learn the text as it is written.

Could You Memorize a Modern Translation?

If you truly dislike this translation, you can always use the verse schedule and follow along in your own Bible. But you'll face a few challenges.

A modern Bible will cram everything into paragraph blocks, so you'll lose the critical *visual* reminders of rhythm that you'll find in this book.

Consider typing out the verses and breaking them into rhythmic lines. But don't share what you've typed with anyone, because a modern translation is probably under copyright. (A few translations are freely licensed.)

You may also though a modern translation has easier words, the more "bookish" rhythms are harder to remember.

Enjoy the DRC

I hope I've made the quirks of this translation a bit less mysterious. The DRC does take some getting used to.

The translation in this book is old, but the **oral rhythms** make it easier to remember than modern translations.

I have a dream to learn the original languages and make a new, freely licensed translation that uses modern language but is steeped in rhythms. Until then, oral overtones make the DRC a great choice for learning these stories by heart.

Move With the Rhythms

Here's another way to enter into these Bible rhythms: **moving**.

Remember Marcel Jousse, the French priest who wrote about Bible rhythms back in 1925? Jousse thought that speaking was not enough. You had to physically *move around*.

In his book, the *Oral Style*, a major theme is **gesture**. Jousse describes Middle Eastern schools where the children practically *danced* as they memorized texts.

Today, researchers into oral cultures still explore how people speak, move, and remember.

How can we use movement to memorize these texts? Honestly, I don't know yet. You tell me.

I'd love to move to these verses, but I haven't figured out how. When I try, the movement distracts me. Perhaps each rhythmic line would have to be much longer.

For me, movement in general has never been a strong suit. If you already love moving and dancing, why not try using these rhythms as you speak the verses? If you find a way to move to these verses, let me know! We could have a great new memory tool.

In some cultures, you **move** while you **memorize**. You can try swaying, stomping, or dancing to the rhythms as you speak.

The Palaces of Memory

If you've been learning one verse and reading one lesson per day, your daily set of verses is getting longer, isn't it? Have you surprised anyone yet with how much you know?

Saying a whole story may seem a bit magical. You can start with, "And straightway in the morning," and *keep going*. How could you do this?

In modern times, people are obsessed with computers. But in ancient cultures, that excitement was lavished on their own memories. In the fourth century, St. Augustine of Hippo wrote:

> And I come to the fields and spacious palaces of my memory, where are the treasures of innumerable images, brought into it ... by the senses....
>
> All these doth that great harbor of the memory receive in her numberless secret and inexpressible windings, to be forthcoming, and brought out at need; each entering in by his own gate, and there laid up.

And though my tongue be still, and my throat mute, so can I sing as much as I will...

I discern the breath of lilies from violets, though smelling nothing; and I prefer honey to sweet wine, smooth before rugged, at the time neither tasting nor handling, but remembering only.

These things do I within, in that vast court of my memory. For there are present with me, heaven, earth, sea, and whatever I could think on ... besides what I have forgotten.

There also meet I with myself, and recall myself, and when, where, and what I have done, and under what feelings....

Great is this force of memory, excessive great, O my God; a large and boundless chamber! Who ever sounded the bottom thereof? Yet is this a power of mine, and belongs unto my nature; nor do I myself comprehend all that I am. Therefore is the mind too strait to contain itself....

Great is the power of memory, a fearful thing, O my God, a deep and boundless manifoldness; and this thing is the mind, and this am I myself. What am I then, O my God? What nature am I? A life various and manifold, and exceeding immense.

Behold in the plains, and caves, and caverns of my memory, innumerable and innumerably full of innumerable kinds of things ... over all these do I run, I fly; I dive on this side and on that, as far as I can, and there is no end.

You may have heard of the *Confessions of St. Augustine*, but you might not have known he was so enthusiastic about memory.

(You can read as much more as you like, for free, at gutenberg.org/etext/3296).

Our technology amazes us, but in the end, all our computers are only tools. Our minds will always dwarf their own dreams.

As you learn to remember deliberately, you may feel as if your own "palaces of memory" are slowly lighting up for the first time. Dark caves become shining terraces. Welcome to a new world.

What About Mnemonics?

When you read St. Augustine talk about the "palaces of memory", did it remind you of "memory palaces"? If you've read any memory books lately, you probably remembered this ancient memory trick.

You might be wondering if I'm ever going to get to the *real* "memory techniques". Everything we've learned so far may seem too natural, even simple. Well, here we are. The real memory technique is: don't use memory techniques.

Memory Swans and Palaces

Memory palaces, along with other memory tricks, are still fairly unknown in our culture. Lately, though, they've been slowly gaining in popularity. With the recent bestseller *Moonwalking With Einstein*, by Joshua Foer, as well as niche books by "gurus" like Tony Buzan and Dominic O'Brien, plus *Memorize Your Faith* by Kevin Vost, people in many circles are slowly discovering the quirky little world of mental tricks for memorizing.

These memory tricks boil down to two principles: *mnemonics* and *organizing* those mnemonics.

A *mnemonic* is a *memory prompt*, and it is (in theory) easy to remember. For instance, instead of memorizing the numeral "2", you memorize, say, a swan.

Why would you do this? A swimming swan with a bent neck looks a little like a "2". But a swan is also (in theory) easier and more fun to think about, and thus remember, than that stark, abstract number "2".

Once you make mnemonics, they must be carefully and cleverly *organized*. That lovely swan is no help if it flies off into the darkness of your mental "caves and caverns", and refuses to reappear when you need the third digit of your ATM pin.

The oldest known way to organize your mnemonics may be the "memory palace". Memory palaces date back at least to the ancient Greeks. First, you imagine a real place that you can remember easily, like your bedroom. Then, you imagine storing your mnemonics, in order, in definite spots around your bedroom. Your bed, your dresser, your desk, whatever.

That's it.

Why Mnemonics Do(n't) Work

Do memory palaces work? Sure. You remember the mnemonics, because when you think, "What did I store in my bed?" you magically *see* the mnemonic you put there. It's the same way you remember where you put *real* things, like your shoes or your jacket. You see a mental image of the thing in that spot. It's a brilliant hack, really.

Other organization methods include using "peg words", which are kind of like spots around a memory palace, except easier to forget, and also "chaining" mnemonics together, which is about what it sounds like, except that the chains tend to break.

Perhaps you sense a certain lack of enthusiasm on my part. Shouldn't I be more excited? Can't people store hundreds, thousands, *tens* of thousands of facts?

Kind of. They can store hundreds, thousands, and tens of thousands of *mnemonics*. But how much do they actually think about the things themselves?

The Wrong Way to Memorize the Bible

When I first found out about memory palaces, I got excited. So excited, that I eventually made up a separate mnemonic for every single verse in the Gospel of Mark. That's nearly *seven hundred* unique mnemonics.

As I memorized each verse, I stored the mnemonic in order around my in-laws' house. Each chapter got its own room. I started in the attic, and worked my way down and out to the backyard.

After several months, I had carefully stocked my mental model of that house with about seven hundred imaginary knick-knacks. In fact, I even had a system that let me locate the verse by the actual *number*. I'll spare you the details, but when I wanted a verse, I could navigate to the correct prompt almost every time.

Think about that. I had reliable, *random* access to almost seven hundred facts. If only I'd known about this back when I was earning grades instead of money.

The problem? The prompt instantly told me the *gist* of the verse, what it was about. But making the leap to the actual *words* of the verse didn't always quite work. At best, it took too much effort.

Mnemonic Mistakes

Slowly I realized that I had made three (at least) critical mistakes:

- I didn't believe I could form a clear mental picture of the actual words. Instead, I made a clear mental picture of the mnemonic.

- I postponed actually *thinking* about the verse. I thought I needed to "memorize" first, and get the bare words perfect. I planned to connect the words to rich imagination later. This was exactly backwards. I should have been visualizing *now*, while I spoke the words.

- I shattered the stories into isolated verses. Instead of renewing them together, as stories, I fed the verses separately into a system of randomized flashcards.

This isolation hamstrung my oral memory. I deftly *destroyed* all the oral memory aids that the original composers had carefully crafted: the rhythm, the context, the repetition of key words, and the sense of story, with a beginning, middle, and end. All gone. Exchanged for a bizarre visual prompt.

You Remember What You Think About

It's easy to see why I got confused. Visual mnemonics, especially bizarre ones (like moonwalking with Einstein), are easy to remember. So easy, it seems like we should just make mnemonics for everything, and our memory problems will be solved.

But memory prompts are just that — *prompts*. Prompts should kickstart the thinking you actually want to do. Your mind is designed for far more complexity than chuckling at distinguished physicists in spacesuits.

Here's the ultimate memory trick: **you remember what you think about.**

That's why sports fanatics can remember every score back to their great-grandfather. Film buffs can recite half a movie without even trying. All of us can recognize hundreds of corporate logos, just from navigating a modern landscape. And then there's our memory for songs...

True, we'll tend to forget mediocre athletes, boring movies and bland logos. If people want to be remembered, they have to make an effort. They need to be bright, colorful, exciting, unique, rhythmic, funny, dramatic, whatever. These qualities are precisely what make us more likely to think about them.

Revenge of the Prompts

In my case, I remember my in-laws' house, and hundreds of little knick-knacks. Actually, in many cases, the actual prompt has faded away, but I remember the *place* I had put it: the corner of the bathroom towel rack, the rings of the shower curtain, the bathroom faucet.

This makes sense. The place was real, and burned into my memory from being there. Plus, I had to focus on finding the *place* every time I searched for a verse. The place itself became my mnemonic.

Today, if I go too long without reviewing Mark, the actual words may start to blur. But almost every place can still trigger the *gist* of the verse.

Alas, this connection works both ways.

When I review the words of Mark, they automatically connect *back to these places*. I start the story of the demoniac and the pigs, and think of … a towel rack.

When some people learn about making crazy mnemonics, they worry that these bizarre images will commandeer your brain. Don't worry. They don't take over, any more than the color of your library carpet, your first science fair project, or any of the other billion facts in your mind.

However, this gut fear is a shrewd intuition. You won't think of your crazy mnemonics all the time, but you might find you see them *whenever you recall the verses*. Through patient perseverance, I have expertly connected the possessed pigs to a towel rack.

As I relearn Mark as stories, I'm slowly making real scenes. But it's extra work. I should have baked these scenes into the words as I learned them the first time. Don't make the same mistake.

You remember what you think about.

Focus your energy on the actual words and thoughts you want to remember. Otherwise, you'll memorize prompts, not stories.

The Right Way (If Any) To Use a Memory Palace

Now you know why I waited so long to introduce you to memory palaces and the magical world of mnemonics. They're a powerful, seductive tool. But you have to know when to use them.

Is there *ever* a good time to use a memory palace? Perhaps.

Memory palaces excel at helping us organize abstract information into a *space*. You might use a palace as a *navigational* tool.

For instance, if you learn an entire Gospel, you might use one prompt for each story, or even each chapter. When one story doesn't naturally lead into the next, you could step back and check your prompts to see what comes next.

It seems that this light use wouldn't interfere with your experience of the verses. It could help you avoid skipping or switching stories, if you want to tell them in order.

But I can't be sure yet. It might be better to organize the material by focusing on the "starter phrases", as one author calls them, which begin each story or chapter.

At any rate, you won't need any palaces for the stories you're learning in this book. You'll find that each familiar incident flows naturally into the next.

Are Mnemonics Really That Bad?

It may seem that I've been unduly harsh on mnemonics. Many august intellectuals (including St. Thomas Aquinas) have sung their praises.

The danger, at least for me, has been that mnemonics have distracted me from thinking about the real things.

Of course, I say this as someone who has spent more time using mnemonics than 99.999% of the population. It's quite possible that mnemonics have strengthened my thinking in ways I don't yet realize and appreciate. And I'm sure that mnemonics will always have their uses.

But your mind is exceedingly, almost frighteningly suggestible. If you tell yourself, "I can't remember these words! I need a mnemonic," then you *won't* remember the words. But if you assure yourself that you *can* remember them, you *will*. It takes more than one look, but with practice, you will reach that goal. You will train that skill.

You may not believe in "positive thinking" making much of a difference in the real world. (Although, as you read the Gospels, you may start to wonder whether our modern concept of "positive thinking" overlaps with Christ's incessant insistence that our own "faith" makes us whole.)

But we aren't talking about the outside world. Memorizing happens *inside your head*. In your own head, you *do* make the rules. You either limit yourself, or you set goals and achieve them.

Mnemonics set the bar too low. You're capable of more.

Plus, they're extra work. Why divert your mental energy?

Finally, they're habit-forming. Mnemonics accustom you to thinking in a particular way. You get better at making mnemonics, not necessarily at real thinking.

For many reasons, it seems better to train yourself to observe and think about what you actually want to know. You can do it!

You've Learned How to Learn Verses!

Congratulations! You've learned how to memorize these verses. From now on, you can focus on the verses themselves.

I hope you've found a comfortable daily routine for your learning and recitations. If not, keep experimenting. You'll find a system that works.

Missed Days and "Deadlines"

If you miss a day (or two ... or three ...), don't give up! Pick up where you left off.

The fifteenth chapter of Mark works out so that if you start on Ash Wednesday and learn a verse each day, you'll finish right around Easter. But that doesn't mean you *have* to. If you miss days here and there, don't fret about going a bit past Holy Saturday before you finish.

If you really want to finish by Holy Saturday, you can learn an extra new verse each day until you catch up. But I wouldn't try this until after your first three or four weeks. It's so important not to rush.

Enjoy

Most important of all: *enjoy this*. Don't let learning the living, rhythmic Word of God slide into homework.

I know how easy it is to slip into the homework mindset. I still do it myself. Those are the times to stop and take a break. It's probably better to miss a day entirely than to "power through" with clenched teeth.

On the other hand, I've often experienced a certain inertia in getting started. Sometimes, I only need to say a few verses to get rolling. Then I enter that place of rhythm and imagination where I'm happy to recite.

Enjoy learning these verses!

If you're not in the mood, try to say a few verses anyway. You might slip into a happier place.

But after a few verses, if you're still grinding, stop. Take a break. Try again later.

There's only one more lesson. I suggest you wait to read it until you've learned all the verses in Mark 15.

God bless your Lent!

Keeping What You've Learned

You've done it.

You've memorized more than you ever thought possible. Verse by verse, day by day, week by week, you've laid up texts like treasures. Congratulations.

One task remains. Keep these treasures from slipping away.

First, Keep Repeating

By now, you've said the oldest verses over forty times. You know them very, very well.

But the more recent verses are still fresh. You've only just now learned the last one.

Your first task is to cement the most recent verses. It may feel strange to keep reciting the Passion stories during Easter, but if you don't, these stories will slip away. Each new verse needs to be repeated daily for about two weeks.

Two weeks is an estimate. If we were using "spaced repetition," you would have a complex schedule. But it's simpler to just repeat the last fourteen verses or so every day for two more weeks.

Then, Recite The Stories Once a Month

Meanwhile, get out your calendar for the next year. Mark **one day each month** (perhaps Sunday) to recite Mark 15. Write "Mk 15".

Once a month will be more often than you need. But it's easy to schedule.

Make sure your first scheduled day is no more than a month from today. I don't want you to lose those last few verses.

If you ever get shaky on a story, simply repeat the whole story every day until you're confident again. When you've polished this memory, you can stop reciting it until your next monthly recitation.

Next year, you can probably say the stories every three months. After that, once or twice a year should be plenty. That's how spaced repetition works. Once you've done those frequent early repetitions, you can wait longer and longer as time goes on.

Ready for More?

Learn the Resurrection!

If you liked learning verses during Lent, why not celebrate Easter by learning the Resurrection? Consider *Easter by Heart*, the next book in this series.

Since you've already trained your memory, you'll be able to learn **two verses a day** instead of one. (Not that you have to.)

As you keep learning verses, you can work your way up to three, four, or even five verses a day. Later books in this series will include special techniques for renewing these longer texts.

Use This Book Next Lent

You can also use this book again next Lent. You may choose to learn these verses all over again, renewing your memories with one or two new verses a day.

Or, you may choose to learn one of the other Passion narratives, at the back of this book.

Celebrate What You've Learned

Meanwhile, don't forget to celebrate what you've already done! You've acquired a new superpower! And you've used this power to write the stories of Christ in your heart.

Celebrating may sound cheesy. Embarrassing. But what's the alternative? If we don't savor our hard-won achievements, when will we ever enjoy anything?

So celebrate. You don't have to call the caterers, but you've already thought of something special even as we speak. Do it.

Keep in Touch

And let me know how all this went for you. I'd love to include your success story in future editions.

I'd also love **your feedback**. What worked for you? What didn't? As you know, I've developed this method through plenty of mistakes. I continue to search for more great improvements. The best ideas will come from people like you, who come to the task with fresh minds.

If you can leave your feedback as an **Amazon review**, you'll also help others find this book and learn what you've learned. These reviews make a huge difference.

I look forward to hearing your thoughts. Welcome to the club! Happy Easter!

Bill Powell
bill@howtoremember.biz
LentByHeart.com

Other Passion Narratives

As promised, here are the Passion narratives from the other three Gospels.

This material can easily last you for several Lents! A warning, though: the Gospels are uniquely challenging because they can be so similar. If you learn Mark 15 first, these words will come to mind when you try to learn passages that are almost, but not quite, identical in another Gospel.

I wish I had an easy solution for this, but I don't. I'm still trying to figure out a clean way to avoid conflicting memories. I've considered various methods, such as singing each Gospel to a different tune. Or you could visualize each Gospel differently somehow, perhaps with a different set of "actors".

Learning four overlapping, similar and yet unique prose narratives may be one of the most challenging memory feats you can try!

For now, my best suggestion is to take it slow, and be patient with yourself. Focus on learning one

Gospel at a time. You wouldn't try to learn Spanish and Italian at the same time, right? Don't try to learn Matthew until you're completely solid on Mark.

On the other hand, you will inevitably compare these narratives. It's fascinating to see which incidents occur only in one or two, and which occur in all four.

For instance, all four Gospels tell the story of when, during the capture of Jesus, a disciple takes a sword and cuts off the ear of the servant of the high priest. But only Luke mentions that Jesus actually healed him.

As you pay attention to these differences, you'll notice certain patterns within each evangelist. What do they tend to focus on? What do they leave out? These patterns may help you keep each narrative straight.

John, of course, is the most unique. Where the other Gospels tend to focus on what Jesus did and said, John often also tells us what Jesus was thinking. At the Last Supper, John diverges dramatically. Where the other Gospels have a brief scene, John gives us several chapters, as Jesus talks with his friends on the night before his murder.

This also makes John the longest selection here, almost 240 verses. You might want to stretch this out over multiple Lents. Or, if you build up your skills to where you can learn five new verses a day, you could tackle John in around 48 days, roughly the course of a single Lent.

But again, don't rush. Learning by heart is a "slow and steady" kind of race.

Mark 14
Chief Priests, Woman With Ointment
Mark 14:1

Not on the festival day

Now the feast of the pasch
    and of the Azymes
        was after two days:
and the chief priests and the scribes
    sought how they might by some wile
lay hold on him
    and kill him.

But they said:
    Not on the festival day,
lest there should be a tumult
    among the people.

The woman brings ointment

And when he was in Bethania,
    in the house of Simon the leper,
        and was at meat,
there came a woman
    having an alabaster box
of ointment
    of precious spikenard.
And breaking the alabaster box,
    she poured it out
        upon his head.

Now there were some
    that had indignation
        within themselves
and said:
    Why was this waste
        of the ointment made?

For this ointment might have been sold
    for more than three hundred pence
        and given to the poor.
And they murmured
    against her.

Jesus defends the woman

But Jesus said:
    Let her alone.
Why do you molest her?
    She hath wrought a good work upon me.

For the poor you have always with you:
    and whensoever,
        you may do them good:
but me
    you have not always.

She hath done what she could:
    she is come beforehand
to anoint my body
    for the burial.

Amen, I say to you,
    wheresoever this gospel shall be preached
        in the whole world,

that also which she hath done
    shall be told
        for a memorial of her.

Judas goes to priests to betray Jesus

And Judas Iscariot,
    one of the twelve,
went to the chief priests,
    to betray him to them.

Who hearing it were glad:
    and they promised him
        they would give him money.
And he sought
    how he might conveniently
        betray him.

Last Supper

Mark 14:12

Disciples prepare for the paschal meal

Now on the first day of the unleavened bread,
    when they sacrificed the pasch,
the disciples say to him:
    Whither wilt thou that we go
and prepare for thee
    to eat the pasch?

And he sendeth two of his disciples
    and saith to them:
        Go ye into the city;

and there shall meet you a man
    carrying a pitcher of water.
        Follow him.

And whithersoever
    he shall go in,
say to the master of the house,
    The master saith,
        Where is my refectory,
where I may eat the pasch
    with my disciples?

And he will shew you
    a large dining room furnished.
        And there prepare ye for us.

And his disciples went their way
    and came into the city.
And they found as he had told them:
    and they prepared the pasch.

Who will betray Jesus?

And when evening was come,
    he cometh with the twelve.

And when they were at table
    and eating,
Jesus saith:
    Amen I say to you,
one of you that eateth with me
    shall betray me.

But they began to be sorrowful
    and to say to him,
one by one:
    Is it I?

Who saith to them:
    One of the twelve,
who dippeth with me
    his hand in the dish.

"This is my body."

And the Son of man indeed goeth,
    as it is written of him:
but woe to that man
    by whom the Son of man
        shall be betrayed.
It were better for him,
    if that man had not been born.

And whilst they were eating,
    Jesus took bread;
and blessing,
    broke and gave to them
and said:
    Take ye.
        This is my body.

And having taken the chalice,
    giving thanks,
he gave it to them.
    And they all drank of it.

And he said to them:
>   This is my blood of the new testament,
>   which shall be shed for many.

Amen I say to you
>   that I will drink no more
>   of the fruit of the vine
until that day
>   when I shall drink it new
>   in the kingdom of God.

Mount of Olives

Mark 14:26

You will all be scandalized this night

And when they had sung an hymn,
>   they went forth to the mount of Olives.

And Jesus saith to them:
>   You will all be scandalized
>   in my regard this night.
For it is written:
>   I will strike the shepherd,
>   and the sheep shall be dispersed.

But after I shall be risen again,
>   I will go before you into Galilee.

Peter will deny Jesus

But Peter saith to him:
>   Although all shall be scandalized in thee,

yet not I.

And Jesus saith to him:
Amen I say to thee,
today,
even in this night,
before the cock crow twice,
thou shalt deny me thrice.

But he spoke
the more vehemently:
Although I should die together with thee,
I will not deny thee.
And in like manner also
said they all.

Let this hour pass

And they came to a farm
called Gethsemani.
And he saith to his disciples:
Sit you here,
while I pray.

And he taketh
Peter and James and John with him:
and he began to fear
and to be heavy.

And he saith to them:
My soul is sorrowful
even unto death.
Stay you here
and watch.

And when he was gone forward a little,
    he fell flat on the ground:
and he prayed that,
    if it might be,
        the hour might pass from him.

And he saith:
    Abba, Father,
all things are possible to thee:
    remove this chalice from me;
but not what I will,
    but what thou wilt.

        "Couldst thou not watch one hour?"

And he cometh and findeth them sleeping.
    And he saith to Peter:
Simon, sleepest thou?
    Couldst thou not watch one hour?

Watch ye:
    and pray
        that you enter not into temptation.
The spirit indeed is willing,
    but the flesh is weak.

And going away again,
    he prayed,
        saying the same words.

And when he returned,
    he found them again asleep
(for their eyes were heavy):
    and they knew not what to answer him.

And he cometh the third time
    and saith to them:
Sleep ye now and take your rest.
    It is enough.
The hour is come:
    behold
the Son of man shall be betrayed
    into the hands of sinners.

Rise up:
    let us go.
Behold,
    he that will betray me
        is at hand.

Judas brings the mob

And while he was yet speaking,
    cometh Judas Iscariot,
        one of the twelve:
and with him a great multitude
    with swords and staves,
from the chief priests
    and the scribes
        and the ancients.

And he that betrayed him
    had given them a sign, saying:
Whomsoever I shall kiss,
    that is he.
Lay hold on him:
    and lead him away carefully.

And when he was come,
    immediately going up to him
he saith:
    Hail, Rabbi!
        And he kissed him.

But they laid hands on him
    and held him.

A disciple attacks the servant

And one of them that stood by,
    drawing a sword,
struck a servant of the chief priest
    and cut off his ear.

Jesus confronts the mob

And Jesus answering,
    said to them:
Are you come out as to a robber,
    with swords and staves
        to apprehend me?

I was daily with you in the temple teaching:
    and you did not lay hands on me.
But that the scriptures
    may be fulfilled.

Man with the linen cloth

Then his disciples,
    leaving him,
        all fled away.

And a certain young man followed him,
    having a linen cloth cast
      about his naked body.
        And they laid hold on him.

But he, casting off the linen cloth,
    fled from them naked.

Condemned by the High Priest

Mark 14:53

Jesus brought before the high priest

And they brought Jesus
    to the high priest.
And all the priests
    and the scribes
      and the ancients
        assembled together.

And Peter followed him afar off,
    even into the court
      of the high priest.
And he sat with the servants
    at the fire
      and warmed himself.

And the chief priests
    and all the council
sought for evidence against Jesus,
    that they might put him to death:
      and found none.

False evidence does not agree

For many bore false witness
        against him:
and their evidences
        were not agreeing.

And some rising up,
        bore false witness against him, saying:

We heard him say,
        I will destroy this temple
                made with hands
and within three days
        I will build another
                not made with hands.

And their witness
        did not agree.

Jesus says, I AM.

And the high priest
        rising up in the midst,
                asked Jesus, saying:
Answerest thou nothing
        to the things that are laid to thy charge
                by these men?

But he held his peace
        and answered nothing.
Again the high priest asked him
        and said to him:
Art thou the Christ

the Son of the Blessed God?

And Jesus said to him:
    I am.
And you shall see the Son of man
    sitting on the right hand
        of the power of God
and coming with the clouds
    of heaven.

Then the high priest
    rending his garments,
saith:
    What need we
        any further witnesses?

You have heard the blasphemy.
    What think you?
Who all condemned him
    to be guilty of death.

And some began to spit on him
    and to cover his face
and to buffet him
    and to say unto him:
        Prophesy.
And the servants struck him
    with the palms their hands.

Peter denies Jesus

Now when Peter was in the court below,
    there cometh one of the maidservants
        of the high priest.

And when she had seen Peter
    warming himself
looking on him,
    she saith:
        Thou also wast with Jesus of Nazareth.

But he denied,
    saying:
I neither know nor understand
    what thou sayest.
And he went forth before the court;
    and the cock crew.

And again
    a maidservant seeing him,
began to say to the standers by:
    This is one of them.

But he denied
    again.
And after a while
    they that stood by
        said again to Peter:
Surely thou art one of them;
    for thou art also a Galilean.

But he began to curse
    and to swear, saying:
I know not this man
    of whom you speak.

And immediately the cock
    crew again.
And Peter remembered the word

that Jesus had said unto him:
Before the cock crow twice,
thou shalt thrice deny me.
And he began to weep,

Matthew 26
Chief Priests, Woman With Ointment
Matthew 26:1

Priests and ancients plot against Jesus

AND it came to pass,
when Jesus had ended all these words,
he said to his disciples:

You know that after two days
shall be the pasch,
and the son of man shall be delivered up
to be crucified:

Then were gathered together
the chief priests and ancients
of the people
into the court of the high priest,
who was called Caiphas:

And they consulted together,
that by subtlety
they might apprehend Jesus,
and put him to death.

But they said:
Not on the festival day,

lest perhaps there should be a tumult
    among the people.

Woman with the ointment

And when Jesus was in Bethania,
    in the house of Simon the leper,

There came to him a woman
    having an alabaster box
        of precious ointment,
and poured it on his head
    as he was at table.

And the disciples seeing it,
    had indignation, saying:
        To what purpose is this waste?

For this might have been sold for much,
    and given to the poor.

And Jesus knowing it,
    said to them:
Why do you trouble this woman?
    for she hath wrought a good work
        upon me.

For the poor you have always with you:
    but me you have not always.

For she in pouring this ointment
    upon my body,
        hath done it for my burial.

Amen I say to you,
    wheresoever this gospel shall be preached
        in the whole world,
that also which she hath done,
    shall be told for a memory of her.

Judas meets with the priests to betray Jesus

Then went one of the twelve,
    who was called Judas Iscariot,
        to the chief priests,

And said to them:
    What will you give me,
        and I will deliver him unto you?
But they appointed him
    thirty pieces of silver.

And from thenceforth
    he sought opportunity
        to betray him.

Last Supper

Matthew 26:17

Disciples prepare for the paschal meal

And on the first day of the Azymes,
    the disciples came to Jesus, saying:
Where wilt thou
    that we prepare for thee
        to eat the pasch?

But Jesus said:
>   Go ye into the city to a certain man,
>   and say to him:
the master saith,
>   My time is near at hand,
with thee I make the pasch
>   with my disciples.

And the disciples did
>   as Jesus appointed to them,
>   and they prepared the pasch.

Who will betray Jesus?

But when it was evening,
>   he sat down with his twelve disciples.

And whilst they were eating,
>   he said:
Amen I say to you,
>   that one of you is about
>   to betray me.

And they being very much troubled,
>   began every one to say:
>   Is it I, Lord?

But he answering, said:
>   He that dippeth his hand
>   with me in the dish,
>   he shall betray me.

The Son of man indeed goeth,
>   as it is written of him:

but woe to that man
    by whom the Son of man
        shall be betrayed:
it were better for him,
    if that man had not been born.

And Judas that betrayed him,
    answering, said:
        Is it I, Rabbi?
He saith to him:
    Thou hast said it.

"This is my body."

And whilst they were at supper,
    Jesus took bread,
        and blessed, and broke:
and gave to his disciples,
    and said:
Take ye, and eat.
    This is my body.

And taking the chalice,
    he gave thanks,
and gave to them, saying:
    Drink ye all of this.

For this is my blood
    of the new testament,
which shall be shed for many
    unto remission of sins.

And I say to you,
    I will not drink from henceforth

of this fruit of the vine,
until that day
when I shall drink it with you new
in the kingdom of my Father.

Mount of Olives

Matthew 26:30

You will all be scandalized this night

And a hymn being said,
they went out unto mount Olivet.

Then Jesus said to them:
All you shall be scandalized
in me this night.
For it is written:
I will strike the shepherd,
and the sheep of the flock
shall be dispersed.

But after I shall be risen again,
I will go before you into Galilee.

Peter will deny Jesus

And Peter answering,
said to him:
Although all shall be scandalized in thee,
I will never be scandalized.

Jesus said to him:
Amen I say to thee,

that in this night
　　before the cock crow,
　　　　thou wilt deny me thrice.

Peter saith to him:
　　Yea, though I should die with thee,
　　　　I will not deny thee.
And in like manner
　　said all the disciples.

"Let this chalice pass from me."

Then Jesus came with them
　　into a country place
　　　　which is called Gethsemani;
and he said to his disciples:
　　Sit you here,
　　　　till I go yonder and pray.

And taking with him Peter
　　and the two sons of Zebedee,
he began to grow sorrowful
　　and to be sad.

Then he saith to them:
　　My soul is sorrowful
　　　　even unto death:
stay you here,
　　and watch with me.

And going a little further,
　　he fell upon his face,
　　　　praying, and saying:
My Father,

if it be possible,
    let this chalice pass from me.
Nevertheless not as I will,
    but as thou wilt.

"Could you not watch one hour?"

And he cometh to his disciples,
    and findeth them asleep,
and he saith to Peter:
    What?
Could you not watch
    one hour with me?

Watch ye, and pray
    that ye enter not into temptation.
The spirit indeed is willing,
    but the flesh weak.

Again the second time,
    he went and prayed, saying:
My Father,
    if this chalice may not pass away,
but I must drink it,
    thy will be done.

And he cometh again
    and findeth them sleeping:
        for their eyes were heavy.

And leaving them,
    he went again:
and he prayed the third time,
    saying the selfsame word.

Judas brings the mob

Then he cometh to his disciples,
    and saith to them:
Sleep ye now
    and take your rest;
behold the hour is at hand,
    and the Son of man shall be betrayed
        into the hands of sinners.

Rise, let us go:
    behold he is at hand
        that will betray me.

As he yet spoke,
    behold Judas, one of the twelve,
        came,
and with him a great multitude
    with swords and clubs,
sent from the chief priests
    and the ancients of the people.

And he that betrayed him,
    gave them a sign, saying:
Whomsoever I shall kiss,
    that is he,
        hold him fast.

And forthwith coming to Jesus,
    he said:
Hail, Rabbi.
    And he kissed him.

And Jesus said to him:
    Friend, whereto art thou come?
Then they came up,
    and laid hands on Jesus,
        and held him.

A disciple attacks the servant

And behold one of them that were with Jesus,
    stretching forth his hand,
        drew out his sword:
and striking the servant
    of the high priest,
        cut off his ear.

Then Jesus saith to him:
    Put up again
        thy sword into its place:
for all that take the sword
    shall perish with the sword.

Thinkest thou that I cannot ask my Father,
    and he will give me presently
        more than twelve legions of angels?

How then shall the scriptures be fulfilled,
    that so it must be done?

Jesus confronts the mob

In that same hour
    Jesus said to the multitudes:
You are come out as it were
    to a robber

with swords and clubs to apprehend me.
I sat daily with you,
    teaching in the temple,
        and you laid not hands on me.

Now all this was done,
    that the scriptures of the prophets
        might be fulfilled.
Then the disciples
    all leaving him,
        fled.

Condemned by the High Priest

Matthew 26:57

Jesus before Caiphas

But they holding Jesus
    led him to Caiphas the high priest,
where the scribes and the ancients
    were assembled.

And Peter followed him afar off,
    even to the court of the high priest.
And going in,
    he sat with the servants,
        that he might see the end.

And the chief priests and the whole council
    sought false witness against Jesus,
        that they might put him to death:

And they found not,
      whereas many false witnesses
            had come in.
And last of all
      there came two false witnesses:

And they said:
      This man said,
I am able to destroy
      the temple of God,
and after three days
      to rebuild it.

And the high priest rising up,
      said to him:
Answerest thou nothing
      to the things which these witness
            against thee?

                 Jesus says, I AM

But Jesus
      held his peace.
And the high priest said to him:
      I adjure thee by the living God,
that thou tell us if thou be
      the Christ the Son of God.

Jesus saith to him:
      Thou hast said it.
Nevertheless I say to you,
      hereafter you shall see
            the Son of man
sitting on the right hand

of the power of God,
    and coming in the clouds of heaven.

Then the high priest
    rent his garments, saying:
He hath blasphemed;
    what further need have we of witnesses?
Behold, now you have heard
    the blasphemy:
        What think you?
But they answering, said:
    He is guilty of death.

Then did they spit in his face,
    and buffeted him:
and others struck his face
    with the palms of their hands,

Saying:
    Prophesy unto us,
        O Christ,
who is he
    that struck thee?

Peter denies Jesus

But Peter sat without in the court:
    and there came to him a servant maid,
        saying:
Thou also wast with Jesus
    the Galilean.

But he denied before them all,
   saying:
      I know not what thou sayest.

And as he went out of the gate,
   another maid saw him,
and she saith to them
   that were there:
This man also
   was with Jesus of Nazareth.

And again he denied with an oath,
   I know not the man.

And after a little while
   they came that stood by,
and said to Peter:
   Surely thou also
      art one of them;
for even thy speech
   doth discover thee.

Then he began to curse and to swear
   that he knew not the man.
      And immediately the cock crew.

And Peter remembered
   the word of Jesus
      which he had said:
Before the cock crow,
   thou wilt deny me thrice.
And going forth,
   he wept bitterly.

Matthew 27
End of Judas

Matthew 27:1

Judas repents

AND when morning was come,
    all the chief priests and ancients
        of the people
took counsel against Jesus,
    that they might put him to death.

And they brought him bound,
    and delivered him to Pontius Pilate
        the governor.

Then Judas,
    who betrayed him,
seeing that he was condemned,
    repenting himself,
brought back the thirty pieces of silver
    to the chief priests and ancients,

Saying:
    I have sinned in betraying
        innocent blood.
But they said:
    What is that to us?
        look thou to it.

Judas kills himself

And casting down the pieces of silver
   in the temple,
      he departed:
and went and hanged himself
   with an halter.

But the chief priests
   having taken the pieces of silver, said:
It is not lawful
   to put them into the corbona,
because it is the price
   of blood.

And after they had consulted together,
   they bought with them
      the potter's field,
to be a burying place
   for strangers.

For this cause the field
   was called Haceldama,
that is,
   The field of blood,
      even to this day.

Then was fulfilled
   that which was spoken
      by Jeremias the prophet,
saying:
   And they took
      the thirty pieces of silver,
the price of him that was prized,

whom they prized
of the children of Israel.

And they gave them unto
the potter's field,
as the Lord appointed to me.

Condemned by Pilate

Matthew 27:11

Pilate questions Jesus

And Jesus stood before the governor,
and the governor asked him,
saying:
Art thou the king
of the Jews?
Jesus saith to him:
Thou sayest it.

And when he was accused
by the chief priests and ancients,
he answered nothing.

Then Pilate saith to him:
Dost not thou hear
how great testimonies
they allege against thee?

And he answered him
to never a word;
so that the governor wondered
exceedingly.

The people choose Barabbas

Now upon the solemn day
    the governor was accustomed
to release to the people
    one prisoner,
        whom they would.

And he had then
    a notorious prisoner,
        that was called Barabbas.

They therefore
    being gathered together,
Pilate said:
    Whom will you that I release to you,
Barabbas,
    or Jesus
        that is called Christ?

For he knew that for envy
    they had delivered him.

And as he was sitting
    in the place of judgment,
his wife sent to him,
    saying:
Have thou nothing to do
    with that just man;
for I have suffered many things this day
    in a dream
        because of him.

But the chief priests and ancients
    persuaded the people,
that they should ask Barabbas,
    and make Jesus away.

And the governor answering,
    said to them:
Whether will you of the two
    to be released unto you?
But they said,
    Barabbas.

Pilate saith to them:
    What shall I do then
        with Jesus that is called Christ?
They say all:
    Let him be crucified.

The governor said to them:
    Why, what evil hath he done?
But they cried out the more,
    saying:
        Let him be crucified.

And Pilate seeing
    that he prevailed nothing,
        but that rather a tumult was made;
taking water
    washed his hands before the people,
        saying:
I am innocent of the blood
    of this just man;
        look you to it.

And the whole people answering,
    said:
His blood be upon us
    and our children.

Crucifixion

Matthew 27:26

Jesus is tortured

Then he released to them Barabbas,
    and having scourged Jesus,
delivered him unto them
    to be crucified.

Then the soldiers of the governor
    taking Jesus into the hall,
gathered together unto him
    the whole band;

And stripping him,
    they put a scarlet cloak about him.

And platting a crown of thorns,
    they put it upon his head,
        and a reed in his right hand.
And bowing the knee before him,
    they mocked him, saying:
        Hail, king of the Jews.

And spitting upon him,
    they took the reed,
        and struck his head.

And after they had mocked him,
 they took off the cloak from him,
and put on him his own garments,
 and led him away to crucify him.

Jesus is crucified

And going out,
 they found a man of Cyrene,
  named Simon:
him they forced
 to take up his cross.

And they came to the place
 that is called Golgotha,
  which is the place of Calvary.

And they gave him wine to drink
 mingled with gall.
And when he had tasted,
 he would not drink.

And after they had crucified him,
 they divided his garments,
  casting lots;
that it might be fulfilled
 which was spoken by the prophet,
saying:
 They divided my garments
  among them;
and upon my vesture
 they cast lots.

And they sat
   and watched him.

And they put over his head
   his cause written:
THIS IS JESUS
   THE KING OF THE JEWS.

Jesus is reviled

Then were crucified with him
   two thieves:
one on the right hand,
   and one on the left.

And they that passed by,
   blasphemed him,
      wagging their heads,

And saying:
   Vah, thou that destroyest
      the temple of God,
and in three days
   dost rebuild it:
save thy own self:
   if thou be the Son of God,
      come down from the cross.

In like manner also
   the chief priests,
      with the scribes and ancients,
         mocking, said:

He saved others;

himself he cannot save.
If he be the king of Israel,
    let him now come down from the cross,
        and we will believe him.

He trusted in God;
    let him now deliver him
        if he will have him;
for he said:
    I am the Son of God.

And the selfsame thing
    the thieves also,
        that were crucified with him,
          reproached him with.

Jesus dies

Now from the sixth hour
    there was darkness
over the whole earth,
    until the ninth hour.

And about the ninth hour
    Jesus cried with a loud voice,
saying:
    Eli, Eli,
        lamma sabacthani?
that is,
    My God, my God,
        why hast thou forsaken me?

And some that stood there and heard,
    said:

This man calleth Elias.

And immediately one of them running
    took a sponge,
        and filled it with vinegar;
and put it on a reed,
    and gave him to drink.

And the others said:
    Let be, let us see
whether Elias will come
    to deliver him.

And Jesus again crying
    with a loud voice,
        yielded up the ghost.

Earthquakes and rising saints

And behold the veil of the temple
    was rent in two
from the top
    even to the bottom,
and the earth quaked,
    and the rocks were rent.

And the graves were opened:
    and many bodies of the saints
        that had slept arose,

And coming out of the tombs
    after his resurrection,
came into the holy city,
    and appeared to many.

Now the centurion
    and they that were with him
        watching Jesus,
having seen the earthquake,
    and the things that were done,
        were sore afraid,
saying:
    Indeed this was the Son of God.

Women who looked on

And there were there many women afar off,
    who had followed Jesus from Galilee,
        ministering unto him:

Among whom was Mary Magdalen,
    and Mary the mother of James and Joseph,
        and the mother of the sons of Zebedee.

Burial

Matthew 27:57

Joseph of Arimathea

And when it was evening,
    there came a certain rich man of Arimathea,
        named Joseph,
who also himself
    was a disciple of Jesus.

He went to Pilate,
    and asked the body of Jesus.
Then Pilate commanded

that the body should be delivered.

Jesus is buried

And Joseph taking the body,
    wrapped it up in a clean linen cloth.

And laid it in his own new monument,
    which he had hewed out in a rock.
And he rolled a great stone
    to the door of the monument,
        and went his way.

And there was there Mary Magdalen,
    and the other Mary
        sitting over against the sepulchre.

The tomb is guarded

And the next day,
    which followed the day of preparation,
the chief priests and the Pharisees
    came together to Pilate,

Saying:
    Sir, we have remembered,
that that seducer said,
    while he was yet alive:
After three days
    I will rise again.

Command therefore the sepulchre
    to be guarded until the third day:
lest perhaps his disciples come

and steal him away,
and say to the people:
    He is risen from the dead;
and the last error
    shall be worse than the first.

Pilate saith to them:
    You have a guard;
        go, guard it as you know.

And they departing,
    made the sepulchre sure,
sealing the stone,
    and setting guards.

Luke 22
Judas Betrays Jesus
Luke 22:1

Judas meets with the priests

NOW the feast of unleavened bread,
    which is called the pasch,
        was at hand.

And the chief priests and the scribes
    sought how they might put Jesus to death:
        but they feared the people.

And Satan entered into Judas,
    who was surnamed Iscariot,
        one of the twelve.

And he went, and discoursed
    with the chief priests and the magistrates,
        how he might betray him to them.

And they were glad,
    and covenanted to give him money.

And he promised.
    And he sought opportunity to betray him
        in the absence of the multitude.

Last Supper

Luke 22:7

Peter and John prepare the paschal meal

And the day of the unleavened bread came,
    on which it was necessary
        that the pasch should be killed.

And he sent Peter and John, saying:
    Go, and prepare for us the pasch,
        that we may eat.

But they said:
    Where wilt thou that we prepare?

And he said to them:
    Behold, as you go into the city,
there shall meet you a man
    carrying a pitcher of water:
follow him into the house
    where he entereth in.

And you shall say
    to the goodman of the house:
The master saith to thee,
    Where is the guest chamber,
where I may eat the pasch
    with my disciples?

And he will shew you
    a large dining room, furnished;
      and there prepare.

And they going,
    found as he had said to them,
      and made ready the pasch.

"This is my body"

And when the hour was come,
    he sat down,
      and the twelve apostles with him.

And he said to them:
    With desire I have desired
to eat this pasch with you,
    before I suffer.

For I say to you,
    that from this time
      I will not eat it,
till it be fulfilled
    in the kingdom of God.

And having taken the chalice,
    he gave thanks,

and said:
    Take, and divide it among you:

For I say to you,
    that I will not drink
        of the fruit of the vine,
            till the kingdom of God come.

And taking bread,
    he gave thanks,
        and brake;
            and gave to them,
saying:
    This is my body,
        which is given for you.
Do this for a commemoration
    of me.

In like manner the chalice also,
    after he had supped,
saying:
    This is the chalice,
the new testament in my blood,
    which shall be shed for you.

Who will betray Jesus?

But yet behold,
    the hand of him that betrayeth me
        is with me on the table.

And the Son of man indeed goeth,
    according to that
        which is determined:

but yet,
    woe to that man
        by whom he shall be betrayed.

And they began to inquire among themselves,
    which of them it was
        that should do this thing.

Who is greatest?

And there was also a strife amongst them,
    which of them should seem
        to be the greater.

And he said to them:
    The kings of the Gentiles
        lord it over them;
and they that have power over them,
    are called beneficent.

But you not so:
    but he that is the greater among you,
        let him become as the younger;
and he that is the leader,
    as he that serveth.

For which is greater,
    he that sitteth at table,
        or he that serveth?
Is it not he
    that sitteth at table?
But I am in the midst of you,
    as he that serveth:

And you are they
    who have continued with me
        in my temptations:

And I dispose to you,
    as my Father hath disposed to me,
        a kingdom;

That you may eat and drink at my table,
    in my kingdom:
and may sit upon thrones,
    judging the twelve tribes of Israel.

Peter will deny Jesus

And the Lord said:
    Simon, Simon,
behold Satan hath desired to have you,
    that he may sift you as wheat:

But I have prayed for thee,
    that thy faith fail not:
and thou,
    being once converted,
        confirm thy brethren.

Who said to him:
    Lord, I am ready to go with thee,
both into prison,
    and to death.

And he said:
    I say to thee, Peter,
the cock shall not crow this day,

till thou thrice deniest
  that thou knowest me.
And he said to them:
  When I sent you without purse,
and scrip,
  and shoes,
    did you want anything?

But they said:
  Nothing.
Then said he unto them:
  But now he that hath a purse,
    let him take it,
      and likewise a scrip;
and he that hath not,
  let him sell his coat,
    and buy a sword.

For I say to you,
  that this that is written
    must yet be fulfilled in me:
And with the wicked
  was he reckoned.
For the things concerning me
  have an end.

But they said:
  Lord, behold
    here are two swords.
And he said to them,
  It is enough.

Mount of Olives

Luke 22:39

"Remove this chalice from me"

And going out,
    he went,
according to his custom,
    to the mount of Olives.
        And his disciples also followed him.

And when he was come to the place,
    he said to them:
Pray,
    lest ye enter
        into temptation.

And he was withdrawn away from them
    a stone's cast;
and kneeling down,
    he prayed,

Saying:
    Father, if thou wilt,
        remove this chalice from me:
but yet not my will,
    but thine be done.

And there appeared to him
    an angel from heaven,
        strengthening him.
And being in an agony,
    he prayed the longer.

And his sweat became as drops of blood,
    trickling down upon the ground.

And when he rose up from prayer,
    and was come to his disciples,
        he found them sleeping for sorrow.

And he said to them:
    Why sleep you?
arise, pray,
    lest you enter into temptation.

Judas brings the mob

As he was yet speaking,
    behold a multitude;
and he that was called Judas,
    one of the twelve,
went before them,
    and drew near to Jesus,
        for to kiss him.

And Jesus said to him:
    Judas, dost thou betray the Son of man
        with a kiss?

A disciple attacks the servant

And they that were about him,
    seeing what would follow,
said to him:
    Lord,
        shall we strike with the sword?

And one of them struck the servant
       of the high priest,
              and cut off his right ear.

But Jesus answering,
       said:
              Suffer ye thus far.
And when he had touched his ear,
       he healed him.

Jesus confronts the mob

And Jesus said to the chief priests,
       and magistrates of the temple,
and the ancients,
       that were come unto him:
Are ye come out,
       as it were against a thief,
              with swords and clubs?

When I was daily with you in the temple,
       you did not stretch forth
              your hands against me:
but this is your hour,
       and the power of darkness.

Condemned by the High Priest

Luke 22:54

Peter denies Jesus

And apprehending him,
       they led him to the high priest's house.

But Peter followed
    afar off.

And when they had kindled a fire
    in the midst of the hall,
and were sitting about it,
    Peter was in the midst of them.

Whom when a certain servant maid had seen
    sitting at the light,
        and had earnestly beheld him,
she said:
    This man also was with him.

But he denied him,
    saying:
        Woman, I know him not.

And after a little while,
    another seeing him, said:
        Thou also art one of them.
But Peter said:
    O man, I am not.

And after the space,
    as it were of one hour,
        another certain man affirmed,
saying:
    Of a truth,
        this man was also with him;
for he is also
    a Galilean.

And Peter said:
    Man, I know not what thou sayest.
And immediately,
    as he was yet speaking,
        the cock crew.

And the Lord turning
    looked on Peter.
And Peter remembered
    the word of the Lord,
        as he had said:
Before the cock crow,
    thou shalt deny me thrice.

And Peter going out,
    wept bitterly.

Jesus is tortured by the servants

And the men that held him,
    mocked him,
        and struck him.

And they blindfolded him,
    and smote his face.
And they asked him, saying:
    Prophesy,
        who is it that struck thee?

And blaspheming,
    many other things
        they said against him.

Jesus is the Son of God

And as soon as it was day,
    the ancients of the people,
and the chief priests
    and scribes,
        came together;
and they brought him
    into their council,
saying:
    If thou be the Christ,
        tell us.

And he saith to them:
    If I shall tell you,
        you will not believe me.

And if I shall also ask you,
    you will not answer me,
        nor let me go.

But hereafter the Son of man
    shall be sitting on the right hand
        of the power of God.

Then said they all:
    Art thou then the Son of God?
Who said:
    You say that I am.

And they said:
    What need we any further testimony?
for we ourselves have heard it
    from his own mouth.

Luke 23
Condemned by Pilate

Luke 23:1

Pilate questions Jesus

AND the whole multitude of them
    rising up,
        led him to Pilate.

And they began to accuse him, saying:
    We have found this man
        perverting our nation,
and forbidding to give tribute
    to Cæsar,
and saying that he
    is Christ the king.

And Pilate asked him, saying:
    Art thou the king of the Jews?
But he answering, said:
    Thou sayest it.

And Pilate said to the chief priests
    and to the multitudes:
        I find no cause in this man.

But they were more earnest,
    saying:
        He stirreth up the people,
teaching throughout all Judea,
    beginning from Galilee to this place.

Jesus before Herod

But Pilate hearing Galilee,
    asked if the man were of Galilee?

And when he understood
    that he was of Herod's jurisdiction,
he sent him away to Herod,
    who was also himself at Jerusalem,
        in those days.

And Herod,
    seeing Jesus,
        was very glad;
for he was desirous of a long time
    to see him,
because he had heard many things of him;
    and he hoped to see some sign
        wrought by him.

And he questioned him in many words.
    But he answered him nothing.

And the chief priests and the scribes stood by,
    earnestly accusing him.

And Herod with his army
    set him at nought,
        and mocked him,
putting on him a white garment,
    and sent him back to Pilate.

And Herod and Pilate were made friends,
    that same day;

for before they were enemies
   one to another.

Pilate tries to release Jesus

And Pilate,
   calling together the chief priests,
and the magistrates,
   and the people,

Said to them:
   You have presented unto me this man,
      as one that perverteth the people;
and behold I,
   having examined him before you,
      find no cause in this man,
in those things wherein
   you accuse him.

No, nor Herod neither.
   For I sent you to him,
and behold,
   nothing worthy of death
      is done to him.

I will chastise him therefore,
   and release him.

The mob demand crucifixion

Now of necessity
   he was to release unto them
      one upon the feast day.

But the whole multitude together
    cried out, saying:
Away with this man,
    and release unto us Barabbas:

Who, for a certain sedition
    made in the city,
and for a murder,
      was cast into prison.

And Pilate again spoke to them,
    desiring to release Jesus.

But they cried again, saying:
    Crucify him,
      crucify him.

And he said to them the third time:
    Why, what evil hath this man done?
I find no cause of death in him.
    I will chastise him therefore,
      and let him go.

But they were instant with loud voices,
    requiring that he might be crucified;
      and their voices prevailed.

And Pilate gave sentence
    that it should be as they required.

And he released unto them him
    who for murder and sedition,
      had been cast into prison,
whom they had desired;

but Jesus he delivered up
    to their will.

Crucifixion

Luke 23:26

Simon of Cyrene, Daughters of Jerusalem

And as they led him away,
    they laid hold of one Simon of Cyrene,
        coming from the country;
and they laid the cross on him
    to carry after Jesus.

And there followed him
    a great multitude of people,
        and of women,
who bewailed
    and lamented him.

But Jesus turning to them, said:
    Daughters of Jerusalem,
        weep not over me;
but weep for yourselves,
    and for your children.

For behold,
    the days shall come,
wherein they will say:
    Blessed are the barren,
and the wombs that have not borne,
    and the paps that have not given suck.

Then shall they begin to say
    to the mountains:
        Fall upon us;
and to the hills:
    Cover us.

For if in the green wood
    they do these things,
what shall be done
    in the dry?

Jesus is crucified

And there were also
    two other malefactors
led with him
    to be put to death.

And when they were come to the place
    which is called Calvary,
they crucified him there;
    and the robbers,
one on the right hand,
    and the other on the left.

And Jesus said:
    Father, forgive them,
        for they know not what they do.
But they,
    dividing his garments,
        cast lots.

Jesus is reviled

And the people stood beholding,
    and the rulers with them derided him,
saying:
    He saved others;
        let him save himself,
if he be Christ,
    the elect of God.

And the soldiers also mocked him,
    coming to him,
        and offering him vinegar,

And saying:
    If thou be the king of the Jews,
        save thyself.

And there was also a superscription
    written over him
in letters of Greek,
    and Latin,
        and Hebrew:
THIS IS THE KING
    OF THE JEWS.

The Good Thief

And one of those robbers who were hanged,
    blasphemed him,
saying:
    If thou be Christ,
        save thyself and us.

But the other answering,
    rebuked him,
saying:
    Neither dost thou fear God,
seeing thou art condemned
    under the same condemnation?

And we indeed justly,
    for we receive
        the due reward of our deeds;
but this man hath done
    no evil.

And he said to Jesus:
    Lord, remember me
        when thou shalt come into thy kingdom.

And Jesus said to him:
    Amen I say to thee,
this day thou shalt be with me
    in paradise.

Jesus dies

And it was almost the sixth hour;
    and there was darkness over all the earth
        until the ninth hour.

And the sun was darkened,
    and the veil of the temple
        was rent in the midst.

And Jesus crying out
    with a loud voice, said:

Father,
    into thy hands
        I commend my spirit.
And saying this,
    he gave up the ghost.

Now the centurion,
    seeing what was done,
glorified God, saying:
    Indeed this was a just man.

And all the multitude of them
    that were come together to that sight,
and saw the things that were done,
    returned striking their breasts.

And all his acquaintance,
    and the women that had followed him
        from Galilee,
stood afar off,
    beholding these things.

Burial

Luke 23:50

Joseph of Arimathea

And behold there was a man named Joseph,
    who was a counsellor,
        a good and just man,

(The same had not consented
    to their counsel and doings;)

of Arimathea,
    a city of Judea;
who also himself looked
    for the kingdom of God.

This man went to Pilate,
    and begged the body of Jesus.

Jesus is buried

And taking him down,
    he wrapped him in fine linen,
and laid him in a sepulchre
    that was hewed in stone,
wherein never yet any man
    had been laid.

And it was the day of the Parasceve,
    and the sabbath drew on.

And the women
    that were come with him from Galilee,
following after,
    saw the sepulchre,
        and how his body was laid.

And returning,
    they prepared spices and ointments;
and on the sabbath day they rested,
    according to the commandment.

John 13
Last Supper
John 13:1

Jesus knows his hour has come

BEFORE the festival day
    of the pasch,
Jesus knowing
    that his hour was come,
that he should pass out of this world
    to the Father:
having loved his own
    who were in the world,
        he loved them unto the end.

And when supper was done,
    (the devil having now put
        into the heart
of Judas Iscariot,
    the son of Simon,
        to betray him,)

Knowing that the Father had given him
    all things into his hands,
and that he came from God,
    and goeth to God;

Jesus washes their feet

He riseth from supper,
    and layeth aside his garments,
and having taken a towel,

girded himself.

After that,
    he putteth water into a basin,
and began to wash the feet
    of the disciples,
and to wipe them with the towel
    wherewith he was girded.

He cometh therefore
    to Simon Peter.
And Peter saith to him:
    Lord, dost thou wash my feet?

Jesus answered,
    and said to him:
What I do thou knowest not now;
    but thou shalt know hereafter.

Peter saith to him:
    Thou shalt never wash my feet.
Jesus answered him:
    If I wash thee not,
        thou shalt have no part with me.

Simon Peter saith to him:
    Lord, not only my feet,
        but also my hands and my head.

Jesus saith to him:
    He that is washed,
needeth not
    but to wash his feet,
        but is clean wholly.

And you are clean,
    but not all.

For he knew who he was
    that would betray him;
therefore he said:
    You are not all clean.

"I have given you an example"

Then after he had washed their feet,
    and taken his garments,
being set down again,
    he said to them:
Know you
    what I have done to you?

You call me Master,
    and Lord;
and you say well,
    for so I am.

If then I being
    your Lord and Master,
        have washed your feet;
you also ought to wash
    one another's feet.

For I have given you an example,
    that as I have done to you,
        so you do also.

Amen, amen I say to you:
    The servant is not greater

than his lord;
neither is the apostle greater
    than he that sent him.

If you know these things,
    you shall be blessed
        if you do them.

I speak not of you all:
    I know whom I have chosen.
But that the scripture
    may be fulfilled:
He that eateth bread with me,
    shall lift up his heel against me.

At present I tell you,
    before it come to pass:
that when it shall come to pass,
    you may believe that I am he.

Amen, amen I say to you,
    he that receiveth whomsoever I send,
        receiveth me;
and he that receiveth me,
    receiveth him that sent me.

Who will betray Jesus?

When Jesus had said these things,
    he was troubled in spirit;
and he testified, and said:
    Amen, amen I say to you,
        one of you shall betray me.

The disciples therefore
    looked one upon another,
        doubting of whom he spoke.

Now there was leaning on Jesus' bosom
    one of his disciples,
        whom Jesus loved.

Simon Peter therefore beckoned to him,
    and said to him:
Who is it
    of whom he speaketh?

He therefore,
    leaning on the breast of Jesus,
saith to him:
    Lord, who is it?

Judas takes the morsel

Jesus answered:
    He it is to whom
        I shall reach bread dipped.
And when he had dipped the bread,
    he gave it to Judas Iscariot,
        the son of Simon.

And after the morsel,
    Satan entered into him.
And Jesus said to him:
    That which thou dost,
        do quickly.

Now no man at the table knew

> to what purpose he said this
> > unto him.

For some thought,
> because Judas had the purse,
that Jesus had said to him:
> Buy those things which we have need of
> > for the festival day:
or that he should give something
> to the poor.

He therefore having received the morsel,
> went out immediately.
> > And it was night.

> *"Love one another, as I have loved you"*

When he therefore
> was gone out,
Jesus said:
> Now is the Son of man glorified,
> > and God is glorified in him.

If God be glorified in him,
> God also will glorify him in himself;
> > and immediately will he glorify him.

Little children,
> yet a little while I am with you.
You shall seek me;
> and as I said to the Jews:
Whither I go you cannot come;
> so I say to you now.

A new commandment I give unto you:
    That you love one another,
as I have loved you,
    that you also love one another.

By this shall all men know
    that you are my disciples,
        if you have love one for another.

Peter will deny Jesus

Simon Peter saith to him:
    Lord, whither goest thou?
Jesus answered:
    Whither I go,
        thou canst not follow me now;
but thou shalt follow
    hereafter.

Peter saith to him:
    Why cannot I follow thee now?
        I will lay down my life for thee.

Jesus answered him:
    Wilt thou lay down thy life for me?
Amen, amen I say to thee,
    the cock shall not crow,
        till thou deny me thrice.

John 14
Last Supper, Continued
John 14:1

"I am the way"

LET not your heart be troubled.
    You believe in God,
        believe also in me.

In my Father's house
    there are many mansions.
If not, I would have told you:
    because I go to prepare a place for you.

And if I shall go,
    and prepare a place for you,
I will come again,
    and will take you to myself;
that where I am,
    you also may be.

And whither I go you know,
    and the way you know.

Thomas saith to him:
    Lord, we know not whither thou goest;
        and how can we know the way?

Jesus saith to him:
    I am the way,
        and the truth,
            and the life.

No man cometh to the Father,
    but by me.

If you had known me,
    you would without doubt
        have known my Father also:
and from henceforth you shall know him,
    and you have seen him.

"Show us the Father"

Philip saith to him:
    Lord, shew us the Father,
        and it is enough for us.

Jesus saith to him:
    Have I been so long a time with you;
        and have you not known me?
Philip, he that seeth me
    seeth the Father also.
How sayest thou,
    Shew us the Father?

Do you not believe,
    that I am in the Father,
        and the Father in me?
The words that I speak to you,
    I speak not of myself.
But the Father who abideth in me,
    he doth the works.

Believe you not
    that I am in the Father,
        and the Father in me?

"Whatsoever you ask"

Otherwise believe
    for the very works' sake.
Amen, amen I say to you,
    he that believeth in me,
the works that I do,
    he also shall do;
        and greater than these shall he do.

Because I go
    to the Father:
and whatsoever you shall ask the Father
    in my name,
        that will I do:
that the Father may be glorified
    in the Son.

If you shall ask me any thing in my name,
    that I will do.

If you love me,
    keep my commandments.

The coming of the Paraclete

And I will ask the Father,
    and he shall give you another Paraclete,
        that he may abide with you for ever.

The spirit of truth,
    whom the world cannot receive,
because it seeth him not,
    nor knoweth him:

but you shall know him;
    because he shall abide with you,
        and shall be in you.

I will not leave you orphans,
    I will come to you.

Yet a little while:
    and the world seeth me no more.
But you see me:
    because I live,
        and you shall live.

In that day you shall know,
    that I am in my Father,
        and you in me,
            and I in you.

He that hath my commandments,
    and keepeth them;
        he it is that loveth me.
And he that loveth me,
    shall be loved of my Father:
and I will love him,
    and will manifest myself to him.

Judas saith to him,
    not the Iscariot:
Lord, how is it,
    that thou wilt manifest thyself to us,
        and not to the world?

Jesus answered,
    and said to him:

If any one love me,
 he will keep my word,
 and my Father will love him,
and we will come to him,
 and will make our abode with him.

He that loveth me not,
 keepeth not my words.
And the word which you have heard,
 is not mine;
  but the Father's who sent me.

These things have I spoken to you,
 abiding with you.

But the Paraclete,
 the Holy Ghost,
whom the Father will send
 in my name,
he will teach you all things,
 and bring all things to your mind,
  whatsoever I shall have said to you.

"Peace I leave with you"

Peace I leave with you,
 my peace I give unto you:
not as the world giveth,
 do I give unto you.
Let not your heart be troubled,
 nor let it be afraid.

You have heard that I said to you:
 I go away,

and I come unto you.
If you loved me,
    you would indeed be glad,
because I go to the Father:
    for the Father is greater than I.

And now I have told you
    before it comes to pass:
that when it shall come to pass,
    you may believe.

I will not now speak
    many things with you.
For the prince of this world cometh,
    and in me he hath not any thing.

But that the world may know,
    that I love the Father:
and as the Father
    hath given me commandment,
        so do I:
Arise,
    let us go hence.

John 15
Last Supper, Continued

John 15:1

"I am the true vine"

I AM the true vine;
    and my Father is the husbandman.

Every branch in me,
    that beareth not fruit,
        he will take away:
and every one that beareth fruit,
    he will purge it,
        that it may bring forth more fruit.

Now you are clean by reason of the word,
    which I have spoken to you.

Abide in me,
    and I in you.
As the branch cannot bear fruit of itself,
    unless it abide in the vine,
so neither can you,
    unless you abide in me.

I am the vine;
    you the branches:
he that abideth in me,
    and I in him,
        the same beareth much fruit:
for without me
    you can do nothing.

If any one abide not in me,
    he shall be cast forth as a branch,
        and shall wither,
and they shall gather him up,
    and cast him into the fire,
        and he burneth.

If you abide in me,
    and my words abide in you,

you shall ask whatever you will,
    and it shall be done unto you.

In this is my Father glorified;
    that you bring forth very much fruit,
        and become my disciples.

"Abide in my love"

As the Father hath loved me,
    I also have loved you.
        Abide in my love.

If you keep my commandments,
    you shall abide in my love;
as I also have kept my Father's commandments,
    and do abide in his love.

These things I have spoken to you,
    that my joy may be in you,
        and your joy may be filled.

This is my commandment,
    that you love one another,
        as I have loved you.

Greater love than this no man hath,
    that a man lay down his life
        for his friends.

"You are my friends"

You are my friends,
    if you do the things that I command you.

I will not now call you servants:
    for the servant knoweth not
        what his lord doth.
But I have called you friends:
    because all things whatsoever
        I have heard of my Father,
            I have made known to you.

You have not chosen me:
    but I have chosen you;
and have appointed you,
    that you should go,
        and should bring forth fruit;
and your fruit should remain:
    that whatsoever you shall ask of the Father
        in my name,
            he may give it you.

These things I command you,
    that you love one another.

"If the world hate you"

If the world hate you,
    know ye,
        that it hath hated me before you.

If you had been of the world,
    the world would love its own:
but because you are not of the world,
    but I have chosen you out of the world,
        therefore the world hateth you.

Remember my word that I said to you:
    The servant is not greater than his master.
If they have persecuted me,
    they will also persecute you:
if they have kept my word,
    they will keep yours also.

But all these things they will do to you
    for my name's sake:
because they know not him
    who sent me.

If I had not come,
    and spoken to them,
        they would not have sin;
but now they have no excuse
    for their sin.

He that hateth me,
    hateth my Father also.

If I had not done among them
    the works that no other man hath done,
        they would not have sin;
but now they have both seen and hated
    both me and my Father.

But that the word may be fulfilled
    which is written in their law:
        They hated me without cause.

But when the Paraclete cometh,
    whom I will send you from the Father,
the Spirit of truth,

who proceedeth from the Father,
he shall give testimony of me.

And you shall give testimony,
because you are with me
from the beginning.

John 16
Last Supper, Continued
John 16:1

Persecutions to come

THESE things have I spoken to you,
that you may not be scandalized.

They will put you out of the synagogues:
yea, the hour cometh,
that whosoever killeth you,
will think that he doth a service to God.

And these things will they do to you;
because they have not known the Father,
nor me.

But these things I have told you,
that when the hour shall come,
you may remember that I told you of them.

But I told you not these things
from the beginning,
because I was with you.
And now I go to him that sent me,

and none of you asketh me:
    Whither goest thou?

But because I have spoken these things to you,
    sorrow hath filled your heart.

"If I go not, the Paraclete will not come"

But I tell you the truth:
    it is expedient to you that I go:
for if I go not,
    the Paraclete will not come to you;
but if I go,
    I will send him to you.

And when he is come,
    he will convince the world of sin,
        and of justice,
            and of judgment.

Of sin:
    because they believed not in me.

And of justice:
    because I go to the Father;
        and you shall see me no longer.

And of judgment:
    because the prince of this world
        is already judged.

I have yet many things to say to you:
    but you cannot bear them now.

But when he,

the Spirit of truth,
    is come,
he will teach you all truth.
    For he shall not speak of himself;
but what things soever he shall hear,
    he shall speak;
and the things that are to come,
    he shall shew you.

He shall glorify me;
    because he shall receive of mine,
        and shall shew it to you.

All things whatsoever the Father hath,
    are mine.
Therefore I said,
    that he shall receive of mine,
        and shew it to you.

"A little while"

A little while,
    and now you shall not see me;
and again a little while,
    and you shall see me:
        because I go to the Father.

Then some of the disciples
    said one to another:
        What is this that he saith to us:
A little while,
    and you shall not see me;
and again a little while,
    and you shall see me,

and,
> because I go to the Father?

They said therefore:
> What is this that he saith,
>> A little while?

we know not
> what he speaketh.

And Jesus knew
> that they had a mind to ask him;

and he said to them:
> Of this do you inquire
>> among yourselves,

because I said:
> A little while,
>> and you shall not see me;

and again a little while,
> and you shall see me?

Amen, amen I say to you,
> that you shall lament and weep,
>> but the world shall rejoice;

and you shall be made sorrowful,
> but your sorrow shall be turned into joy.

A woman, when she is in labour,
> hath sorrow,
>> because her hour is come;

but when she hath brought forth the child,
> she remembereth no more the anguish,

for joy that a man
> is born into the world.

So also you now indeed have sorrow;
    but I will see you again,
and your heart shall rejoice;
    and your joy
        no man shall take from you.

And in that day
    you shall not ask me any thing.
Amen, amen I say to you:
    if you ask the Father any thing
        in my name,
            he will give it you.

"Ask, and you shall receive"

Hitherto you have not asked any thing
    in my name.
Ask, and you shall receive;
    that your joy may be full.

These things I have spoken to you
    in proverbs.
The hour cometh,
    when I will no more speak to you in proverbs,
        but will shew you plainly of the Father.

In that day you shall ask in my name;
    and I say not to you,
        that I will ask the Father for you:

For the Father himself loveth you,
    because you have loved me,
and have believed that I came
    out from God.

I came forth from the Father,
    and am come into the world:
again I leave the world,
    and I go to the Father.

The disciples believe

His disciples say to him:
    Behold, now thou speakest plainly,
        and speakest no proverb.

Now we know that thou knowest all things,
    and thou needest not
        that any man should ask thee.
By this we believe
    that thou camest forth from God.

Jesus answered them:
    Do you now believe?

Behold, the hour cometh,
    and it is now come,
that you shall be scattered
    every man to his own,
        and shall leave me alone;
and yet I am not alone,
    because the Father is with me.

These things I have spoken to you,
    that in me you may have peace.
In the world you shall have distress:
    but have confidence,
        I have overcome the world.

John 17
Last Supper, Concluded
John 17:1

"Glorify thy son"

THESE things Jesus spoke,
    and lifting up his eyes to heaven,
he said:
    Father, the hour is come,
glorify thy Son,
    that thy Son may glorify thee.

As thou hast given him power over all flesh,
    that he may give eternal life
        to all whom thou hast given him.

Now this is eternal life:
    That they may know thee,
        the only true God,
and Jesus Christ,
    whom thou hast sent.

I have glorified thee on the earth;
    I have finished the work
        which thou gavest me to do.

And now glorify thou me,
    O Father,
        with thyself,
with the glory which I had,
    before the world was,
        with thee.

I have manifested thy name
    to the men whom thou hast given me
        out of the world.
Thine they were,
    and to me thou gavest them;
        and they have kept thy word.

Prayer for the disciples, in the world

Now they have known,
    that all things which thou hast given me,
        are from thee:

Because the words which thou gavest me,
    I have given to them;
and they have received them,
    and have known in very deed
        that I came out from thee,
and they have believed
    that thou didst send me.

I pray for them:
    I pray not for the world,
        but for them whom thou hast given me:
            because they are thine:

And all my things are thine,
    and thine are mine;
        and I am glorified in them.

And now I am not in the world,
    and these are in the world,
        and I come to thee.
Holy Father,

keep them in thy name
whom thou has given me;
that they may be one,
as we also are.

While I was with them,
I kept them in thy name.
Those whom thou gavest me have I kept;
and none of them is lost,
but the son of perdition,
that the scripture may be fulfilled.

And now I come to thee;
and these things I speak
in the world,
that they may have my joy
filled in themselves.

I have given them thy word,
and the world hath hated them,
because they are not of the world;
as I also am not of the world.

I pray not that thou shouldst take them
out of the world,
but that thou shouldst keep them
from evil.

They are not of the world,
as I also am not of the world.

Sanctify them in truth.
Thy word is truth.

As thou hast sent me into the world,
  I also have sent them into the world.

And for them do I sanctify myself,
  that they also may be sanctified in truth.

"That they all may be one"

And not for them only do I pray,
  but for them also
who through their word
  shall believe in me;

That they all may be one,
  as thou, Father, in me,
    and I in thee;
that they also may be one in us;
  that the world may believe
    that thou hast sent me.

And the glory which thou hast given me,
  I have given to them;
that they may be one,
  as we also are one:

I in them,
  and thou in me;
that they may be made perfect
  in one:
and the world may know
  that thou hast sent me,
and hast loved them,
  as thou hast also loved me.

Father, I will that where I am,
    they also whom thou hast given me
        may be with me;
that they may see my glory
    which thou hast given me,
because thou hast loved me
    before the creation of the world.

Just Father,
    the world hath not known thee;
but I have known thee:
    and these have known
        that thou hast sent me.

And I have made known thy name to them,
    and will make it known;
that the love wherewith thou hast loved me,
    may be in them,
        and I in them.

John 18
Jesus Is Captured
John 18:1

Judas brings the mob

WHEN Jesus had said these things,
    he went forth with his disciples
over the brook Cedron,
    where there was a garden,
into which he entered
    with his disciples.

And Judas also,
    who betrayed him,
knew the place;
    because Jesus had often resorted thither
        together with his disciples.

Judas therefore having received a band
    of soldiers and servants
        from the chief priests and the Pharisees,
cometh thither with lanterns
    and torches and weapons.

Jesus confronts the mob

Jesus therefore,
    knowing all things
        that should come upon him,
went forth,
    and said to them:
        Whom seek ye?

They answered him:
    Jesus of Nazareth.
Jesus saith to them:
    I am he.
And Judas also,
    who betrayed him,
        stood with them.

As soon therefore
    as he had said to them:
        I am he;
they went backward,
    and fell to the ground.

Again therefore he asked them:
    Whom seek ye?
And they said,
    Jesus of Nazareth.

Jesus answered,
    I have told you that I am he.
If therefore you seek me,
    let these go their way.

That the word might be fulfilled which he said:
    Of them whom thou hast given me,
        I have not lost any one.

Simon Peter attacks the servant

Then Simon Peter,
    having a sword,
drew it,
    and struck the servant of the high priest,
        and cut off his right ear.
And the name of the servant
    was Malchus.

Jesus therefore said to Peter:
    Put up thy sword into the scabbard.
The chalice which my Father hath given me,
    shall I not drink it?

Condemnation by the High Priest
John 18:12

Jesus before Annas

Then the band and the tribune,
    and the servants of the Jews,
took Jesus,
    and bound him:

And they led him away to Annas first,
    for he was father in law to Caiphas,
        who was the high priest of that year.

Now Caiphas was he
    who had given the counsel to the Jews:
That it was expedient that one man
    should die for the people.

Peter denies Jesus

And Simon Peter followed Jesus,
    and so did another disciple.
And that disciple was known to the high priest,
    and went in with Jesus
        into the court of the high priest.

But Peter stood
    at the door without.
The other disciple therefore,
    who was known to the high priest,
        went out,
and spoke to the portress,

and brought in Peter.

The maid therefore that was portress,
    saith to Peter:
Art not thou also
    one of this man's disciples?
He saith:
    I am not.

Now the servants and ministers
    stood at a fire of coals,
because it was cold,
    and warmed themselves.
And with them was Peter also,
    standing, and warming himself.

Annas questions Jesus

The high priest therefore
    asked Jesus of his disciples,
        and of his doctrine.

Jesus answered him:
    I have spoken openly to the world:
I have always taught in the synagogue,
    and in the temple,
        whither all the Jews resort;
and in secret
    I have spoken nothing.

Why asketh thou me?
    ask them who have heard
        what I have spoken unto them:
behold they know

what things I have said.

And when he had said these things,
      one of the servants standing by,
            gave Jesus a blow,
saying:
      Answerest thou the high priest so?

Jesus answered him:
      If I have spoken evil,
            give testimony of the evil;
but if well,
      why strikest thou me?

And Annas sent him bound
      to Caiphas the high priest.

Peter denies Jesus again

And Simon Peter was standing,
      and warming himself.
They said therefore to him:
      Art not thou also one of his disciples?
He denied it,
      and said:
            I am not.

One of the servants of the high priest
      (a kinsman to him
            whose ear Peter cut off)
saith to him:
      Did I not see thee
            in the garden with him?

Again therefore Peter denied;
    and immediately the cock crew.

Condemnation by Pilate

John 18:28

"What accusation bring you?"

Then they led Jesus from Caiphas
    to the governor's hall.
And it was morning;
    and they went not into the hall,
that they might not be defiled,
    but that they might eat the pasch.

Pilate therefore went out to them,
    and said:
What accusation bring you
    against this man?

They answered, and said to him:
    If he were not a malefactor,
        we would not have delivered him up to thee.

Pilate therefore said to them:
    Take him you,
        and judge him according to your law.
The Jews therefore said to him:
    It is not lawful for us
        to put any man to death;

That the word of Jesus might be fulfilled,
    which he said,

signifying what death
    he should die.

"Art thou the king of the Jews?"

Pilate therefore went into the hall again,
    and called Jesus,
and said to him:
    Art thou the king of the Jews?

Jesus answered:
    Sayest thou this thing of thyself,
        or have others told it thee of me?

Pilate answered:
    Am I a Jew?
Thy own nation,
    and the chief priests,
have delivered thee up to me:
    what hast thou done?

Jesus answered:
    My kingdom is not of this world.
If my kingdom were of this world,
    my servants would certainly strive
that I should not be delivered
    to the Jews:
but now my kingdom
    is not from hence.

Pilate therefore said to him:
    Art thou a king then?
Jesus answered:
    Thou sayest that I am a king.

For this was I born,
    and for this came I into the world;
that I should give testimony
    to the truth.
Every one that is of the truth,
    heareth my voice.

"I find no cause in him."

Pilate saith to him:
    What is truth?
And when he said this,
    he went out again to the Jews,
and saith to them:
    I find no cause in him.

But you have a custom
    that I should release one unto you
        at the pasch:
will you, therefore,
    that I release unto you
        the king of the Jews?

Then cried they all again, saying:
    Not this man,
        but Barabbas.
Now Barabbas
    was a robber.

John 19
Condemnation by Pilate, Continued

John 19:1

Jesus is tortured

THEN therefore,
    Pilate took Jesus,
        and scourged him.

And the soldiers platting a crown of thorns,
    put it upon his head;
and they put on him
    a purple garment.

And they came to him,
    and said:
Hail, king of the Jews;
    and they gave him blows.

"Behold the man."

Pilate therefore went forth again,
    and saith to them:
Behold, I bring him forth unto you,
    that you may know
        that I find no cause in him.

(Jesus therefore came forth,
    bearing the crown of thorns
        and the purple garment.)
And he saith to them:
    Behold the Man.

When the chief priests, therefore,
　　and the servants,
　　　　had seen him,
they cried out, saying:
　　Crucify him,
　　　　crucify him.
Pilate saith to them:
　　Take him you,
　　　　and crucify him:
for I find
　　no cause in him.

The Jews answered him:
　　We have a law;
and according to the law
　　he ought to die,
because he made himself
　　the Son of God.

When Pilate therefore
　　had heard this saying,
　　　　he feared the more.

Pilate questions Jesus again

And he entered into the hall again,
　　and he said to Jesus:
　　　　Whence art thou?
But Jesus gave him
　　no answer.

Pilate therefore saith to him:
　　Speakest thou not to me?
knowest thou not

that I have power to crucify thee,
 and I have power to release thee?

Jesus answered:
 Thou shouldst not have any power against me,
  unless it were given thee from above.
Therefore,
 he that hath delivered me to thee,
  hath the greater sin.

"We have no king but Cæsar."

And from henceforth Pilate sought
 to release him.
But the Jews cried out, saying:
 If thou release this man,
  thou art not Cæsar's friend.
For whosoever maketh himself a king,
 speaketh against Cæsar.

Now when Pilate had heard these words,
 he brought Jesus forth,
and sat down in the judgment seat,
 in the place that is called Lithostrotos,
  and in Hebrew Gabbatha.

And it was the parasceve of the pasch,
 about the sixth hour,
and he saith to the Jews:
 Behold your king.

But they cried out:
 Away with him;
  away with him;

crucify him.
Pilate saith to them:
Shall I crucify your king?
The chief priests answered:
We have no king but Cæsar.

Crucifixion

John 19:16

Jesus is crucified

Then therefore
he delivered him to them
to be crucified.
And they took Jesus,
and led him forth.

And bearing his own cross,
he went forth to that place
which is called Calvary,
but in Hebrew Golgotha.

Where they crucified him,
and with him two others,
one on each side,
and Jesus in the midst.

"King of the Jews"

And Pilate wrote a title also,
and he put it upon the cross.
And the writing was:
JESUS OF NAZARETH,

THE KING OF THE JEWS.

This title therefore
    many of the Jews did read:
because the place where Jesus was crucified
    was nigh to the city:
and it was written in Hebrew,
    in Greek,
        and in Latin.

Then the chief priests of the Jews
    said to Pilate:
Write not,
    The King of the Jews;
but that he said,
    I am the King of the Jews.

Pilate answered:
    What I have written,
        I have written.

Soldiers cast lots for his garments

The soldiers therefore,
    when they had crucified him,
        took his garments,
(and they made four parts,
    to every soldier a part,)
        and also his coat.
Now the coat was without seam,
    woven from the top throughout.

They said then one to another:
    Let us not cut it,

but let us cast lots for it,
    whose it shall be;
that the scripture might be fulfilled, saying:
    They have parted my garments among them,
        and upon my vesture they have cast lot.
And the soldiers indeed
    did these things.

"Woman, behold thy son."

Now there stood by the cross of Jesus,
    his mother,
and his mother's sister,
    Mary of Cleophas,
        and Mary Magdalen.

When Jesus therefore had seen his mother
    and the disciple standing
        whom he loved,
he saith to his mother:
    Woman,
        behold thy son.

After that,
    he saith to the disciple:
        Behold thy mother.
And from that hour,
    the disciple took her to his own.

Jesus dies

Afterwards, Jesus knowing that all things
    were now accomplished,
that the scripture might be fulfilled,

said:
    I thirst.

Now there was a vessel set there
    full of vinegar.
And they, putting a sponge
    full of vinegar and hyssop,
        put it to his mouth.

Jesus therefore,
    when he had taken the vinegar, said:
        It is consummated.
And bowing his head,
    he gave up the ghost.

Pierced, not broken

Then the Jews,
    (because it was the parasceve,)
that the bodies might not remain on the cross
    on the sabbath day,
        (for that was a great sabbath day,)
besought Pilate
    that their legs might be broken,
        and that they might be taken away.

The soldiers therefore came;
    and they broke the legs of the first,
        and of the other that was crucified with him.

But after they were come to Jesus,
    when they saw that he was already dead,
        they did not break his legs.

But one of the soldiers
    with a spear opened his side,
and immediately there came out
    blood and water.

And he that saw it,
    hath given testimony,
        and his testimony is true.
And he knoweth that he saith true;
    that you also may believe.

For these things were done,
    that the scripture might be fulfilled:
        You shall not break a bone of him.

And again another scripture saith:
    They shall look on him whom they pierced.

Burial

John 19:38

Joseph of Arimathea

And after these things,
    Joseph of Arimathea
(because he was a disciple of Jesus,
    but secretly for fear of the Jews)
besought Pilate that he might take away
    the body of Jesus.
        And Pilate gave leave.
He came therefore,
    and took the body of Jesus.

And Nicodemus also came,
    (he who at the first
        came to Jesus by night,)
bringing a mixture of myrrh and aloes,
    about an hundred pound weight.

Jesus is buried

They took therefore the body of Jesus,
    and bound it in linen cloths,
        with the spices,
as the manner of the Jews is
    to bury.

Now there was in the place
    where he was crucified,
        a garden;
and in the garden a new sepulchre,
    wherein no man yet had been laid.

There, therefore,
    because of the parasceve of the Jews,
they laid Jesus,
    because the sepulchre was nigh at hand.

Let Me Know

If you decide to learn one of these other narratives, please let me know how it goes! I'm always looking for fresh ideas. Thanks!

Bill Powell
bill@howtoremember.biz
LentByHeart.com

About the Author

Bill Powell has memorized tens of thousands of words, including the entire Gospel of Mark. He explores new ways to think, imagine and remember at **HowToRemember.biz**.

Bill lives in Virginia, in the Shenandoah Valley, with his wife, their four children, and a young forest garden.

Ready to Learn More?

You've learned the Passion. Now keep learning with the **Books by Heart**™ series.

Easter by Heart

Hordes of Christians struggle and groan through six weeks of Lent, shout with relief on Easter Sunday, and then ... forget the whole thing before they finish the Easter candy.

Easter is a *season*, not a single day of egg hunting and festive hats. If you learn just **one new verse each day** through the Easter season, you'll know the **entire Resurrection story from John** by Pentecost.

Read more at **EasterByHeart.com**.

Christmas by Heart

This book offers you an exciting new Advent and Christmas ritual: a daily Christmas verse. Every day, you'll learn a new verse of the Christmas story.

These verses will add up. By the end of the seasons, you'll know *every* Christmas verse we have in the Gospels. And you will have celebrated the *seasons* of Advent and Christmas.

Read more at **ChristmasByHeart.com**.

BooksByHeart.com

BLUE VINE